The Observation of
SAVAGE PEOPLES

The Observation of
SAVAGE PEOPLES
by
JOSEPH-MARIE DÉGERANDO
translated by
F. C. T. MOORE
with a preface by
E. E. EVANS-PRITCHARD

UNIVERSITY OF CALIFORNIA PRESS
Berkeley and Los Angeles   1969

First published 1969 in the United States by
University of California Press
Berkeley and Los Angeles
California

Translated from the French
*Considérations sur les méthodes à suivre dans
l'observation des Peuples Sauvages 1800*

© F. C. T. Moore *1969*

All Rights Reserved

Printed in Great Britain

Contents

Acknowledgements	Page vii
Preface	ix
Documentation	xi
Translator's Introduction	1
Text	59
Sources	105
Index	117

List of Illustrations

	Facing page
Joseph-Marie Degérando	4
Nicolas-Thomas Baudin	5
Louis-François Jauffret	20
François Péron	21

Acknowledgements

The research on which this book is based was made possible by St. Antony's College, Oxford, and by Birmingham University. I owe a debt to present and past friends and colleagues, and especially to the following, whose help and encouragement were, in their various ways, indispensable: Sir Isaiah Berlin, Austin Duncan-Jones, E. E. Evans-Pritchard, Henri Gouhier, Douglas Johnson, Evelyn Lawton, Godfrey Lienhardt, Rodney Needham, Ahmed al-Shahi, Gillian Sinclair.

F.C.T.M.

Preface

I am grateful for the privilege of being associated with this book, but there is no need for me to write more than a brief preface, for the text is perfectly clear and all that requires to be said by way of introduction to it is said by Dr. Moore. We are indebted to him for the rediscovery of Degérando's paper and for his translation of it and his discussion of its significance, for it is a paper of great interest to both anthropologists and students of the history of ideas. It is remarkable that it should have been forgotten for so long: I cannot remember a single reference to it in books dealing with the development of social anthropology.

The idea that anthropology is a natural science which should study human institutions by the same methods of observation and comparison as are employed in the study of physical and organic phenomena was a fairly common notion in the eighteenth century. Where Degérando was original was in recognizing and stating that for the most part observations made by explorers among savages were casual and superficial and did not therefore provide an adequate guide to their customs, and thought: what was needed were detailed studies of primitive peoples such as were not made, on the scale he wanted, till over a century later.

He thought, however, that something might be achieved by giving informed advice to those French expeditions at the time setting forth on their explorations, in which scientific, political, commercial and humanitarian interests were all mixed up. The advice consisted firstly in pointing out the faults of earlier travellers – he must have been well-read in the travel literature of his day – and secondly in listing the topics about which observations should be made, and recommending how they should be made. In doing so, he showed much insight, emphasizing all the major techniques of inquiry which anthropological students now take for granted in conducting their fieldwork, but were first set forth clearly in Degérando's paper. To mention only a few: research over a long period; a knowledge of the native language; participation in the life of the people being studied; sampling; careful checking of information; the conducting of systematic inquiries and the keeping of systematic notes; the collection of vernacular texts; precision in the use of terms; and the study of every aspect of social life, since one set of activities cannot be fully understood without a knowledge of the other. The paper reads as though it might have been written yesterday.

However, nothing came of all this, and the expedition to Australia, for which it was primarily written, was ethnographically speaking a disaster. Degérando was asking too much of explorers with a wide range of other interests, and Dr. Moore may well be right in suggesting that the practical failure of Degérando's paper may also have been due to the decline in French colonial ambitions; for certainly the development of social anthropology in England is linked to the spread of our colonial empire and its administrative, missionary and commercial needs.

E. E. EVANS-PRITCHARD

Documentation

Full bibliographic details of Degérando's text, which I happened on in the Bibliothèque nationale in Paris, are given in the appropriate place in the bibliography.

No editorial changes have been made: the text is translated as it stands, including the shoulder headings.

The introduction is sparingly documented by footnotes referring to the bibliography, which provides for fuller documentation or further enquiry.

The bibliography is divided into three sections, of unpublished material, primary published sources, and secondary sources. References are made by a section number, and an item number in each section.

Translator's Introduction

I

THERE have been observant travellers from the first. But not anthropologists. It is a distinction that historians of anthropology, scavenging for material, have not always been eager to draw.

At least since the time of Herodotos, we have read interesting and entertaining accounts of the tourist's view of an alien people. Sometimes such accounts have been systematized, yielding answers to various questions. Are all races of men descended from Noah? If so, what is their genealogy? This question, and others like it, have seemed important: and the value of industrious compilations of travellers' tales has been estimated by their capacity to meet such questions. For long, this was the very most system and significance that was expected in a genre of writing which traditionally provided curiosities and entertainment, no more.

But a mark of the anthropologist is his concern for the systematic study of social phenomena. And it is only quite recently that it has occurred to men that other societies can be, in themselves, a proper object of systematic empirical enquiry.

But how recently? Judgment might vary over Malinowski, Frazer, Durkheim, Tylor; but it would be natural to place the pioneer, at earliest, in the second half of the nineteenth century. Certainly, it will be said, the eighth year of the Republic of France is the wrong date for a clear and thorough survey of the errors to avoid, the questions to ask, and the methods to follow in the field-work of an unconceived science. For at any rate in 1800, there was no anthropology.

Yet it was in this year that a young philosopher from Lyons, Joseph-Marie Degérando, as a memoir to serve as guidance to some of the members of the *Société des Observateurs de l'Homme* in an impending expedition to Australia, delivered the text here translated, a text which it would be natural to take as a capital work of anthropology.

A brief summary will tell why. We read first an authoritative list of the faults of previous observations. They were incomplete, superficial, and unsystematic. They were insufficiently verified. They were made out of context, without regard for the interdependence of social facts. They were infected by analogies drawn from our own culture, and not necessarily applicable to that under observation. They were conveyed often in ambiguous or misleading language. They were made by aliens, who, because they did not attempt in any way to become members of the society under observation, were likely to misunderstand it. They failed to give an effective account of the language of that society. They consequently conveyed no insight into its ways of thinking.

This masterly list of eight faults is to be examined in the text. But a mere enumeration is enough to show that Degérando's 'philosophical traveller' is to be the same man as our anthropologist. And such acute awareness of problems of field-work is startling at a time at which there was no such thing. Especially at three points: the warning against extrapolation from our own culture, the recommendation that observers should attempt to participate in the society under observation, the strong emphasis on the study of its language.

The last point is picked up when we turn to Degérando's positive recommendations. Here he says that the first need of all is to understand the language of the people to be observed.

He goes on to recommend what might be regarded as a questionable method for learning such a language from scratch. It is a method which takes the simplest elements of language to be nouns designating the most common and palpable objects, and proceeds by prescribing the use of demonstrative gestures to ascertain such nouns. The rest must be built up on this basis.

It may be argued that this is a false or over-sophisticated method. For it supposes not only that the language to be learnt has a single word for each of the objects pointed out, but also that the informant will understand a demonstrative gesture (such as pointing at a tree) as a request that he should utter the common noun (and not, for example, any proper name) ordinarily used to refer to that object.

It may be argued that language is not in fact learnt, nor should we try to learn it, in such artificial situations of ostensive definition. Its true elements, we may say, are utterances which perform common functions, like calling a person from a group, asking for food, localizing a pain, warning a person not to do the same again. It is by seeing such functions performed by such utterances (above all when we try them ourselves), that we learn the language.

Degérando shows some little recognition of these points, but we may doubt whether he accomplished his 'master-work of philosophy' by giving the right rules for learning an alien language.

For the observer, however, what matters is not how he has learnt the language, but that he has learnt it. And Degérando adds a telling postscript to this section. Other things in a society besides the articulate utterances of its members should be regarded as having meaning. Trophies, civil and religious practices, dances, are just as meaningful as words. The traveller should try to understand the sense attached to them, their effects and their origin.

Such is the emphasis which Degérando gives language and other meaningful social phenomena. Here again, he put his finger surely on a critical point of a science that did not yet exist.

The next step prescribed by the method is the careful observation of the physical nature and circumstances of the people under observation. A detailed list of questions is put before us. We turn then to the observation of the individual 'as an intellectual and moral being'. Once more, an exhaustive list of questions.

But Degérando is doctrinaire again. The received philosophy derived all man's moral and intellectual nature from sensations. Ideas were 'sensations transformed'. So the anthropologist, says Degérando, must first of all make a study of the sensations of the people under observation. How developed and discriminatory are their senses? Which has priority, and which gives most pleasure? Everything will flow from this.

It is a method which might be profitable, but could scarcely be taken as mandatory. Indeed, the recommended order of research would be seriously reduced in value if, as seems likely, the development and capacity of the senses is not an unalterable physiological datum, but is itself, at least in part, a function of social influences. A people which lacks a certain colour word, and which does not make colour distinctions made by us, is not necessarily physiologically incapable of doing so.

We hesitate then to accept this section as it stands. But we are struck by the system and comprehensiveness of the questions posed, and by the perceptive warnings given.

Finally, we turn to what Degérando calls 'a new order of research' – to the study of man in society, to social anthropology properly so called.

Here further questions are proposed – first about family and kinship, and all that relates to them, then about society at large, concerning political, military, legal, economic, moral and religious matters.

Such, very briefly, is the scope of Degérando's recommendations. It is to be observed how well they bear comparison with more modern anthropological

Acad.ᵉ des Inscript.ⁿ et Belles lettres. (Histoire de la Philosophie.)

LE BARON DE GÉRANDO,
(Joseph, Marie.)

Pair de France, Conseiller d'État, Commandeur de la Légion d'honneur,
Professeur à la Faculté de droit de Paris, Secrétaire de la société d'encouragem.ᵗ
pour l'industrie nationale et de la société pour l'Instruction élémentaire.

Né à Lyon, le 29 Février 1772, élu en 1805.

N. BAUDIN,

Capitaine de Vaisseau, Commandant en chef l'Expédition entreprise en l'An IX, pour des recherches relatives aux Sciences et aux Arts, l'un des Correspondans de la Société des Observateurs de l'Homme

De Cook, de Bougainville émule généreux
Sur leurs traces Baudin va marcher à la gloire,
Et, dans les fastes de l'Histoire,
Clio marque déjà sa place à côte d'eux.

Déposé à la Bibliothèque Nationale. *Péron, l'un des Zoologistes de l'Expédition.*

questionnaires.[1] At times, it is true, Degérando suggests that the comparison of one society and another will enable us to strip away the accidents of humanity and reveal its essence. This is the crudest view of the comparative method in anthropology. At times he predicts that the gathering of legend and tradition will make possible a speculative reconstruction of the early history of mankind. At times he has his eye on the cultural pre-eminence, the political glory, or even the commercial advancement of France. But none of this concerns his actual advice to those explorers under the command of Captain Nicolas Baudin. By an earlier judgment, he wrote at a time when there was no anthropology. Enough has now been said to raise a substantial doubt. Was that science after all conceived at that time? And then, if it was, why was it not practised?

II

A hardy, and perhaps a foolhardy commentator would turn to the construction of a massive synthesis of the notion of primitive peoples in eighteenth and nineteenth century European consciousness, would attend to the papers of tourist and administrator, of trader, explorer and missionary, would unearth popular sayings, and the likenesses of savages in art and literature, would consult works of theory and test them against unguarded correspondence, would elicit the structure of a grand historical movement of ideas.

He would be a speculator. For ideas live not in the century-spanning playgrounds of the scholar, but in what people believe and in what they do. So must the document which now concerns us be understood not so much in terms of a scale of antecedents and influences as by a study of what Degérando and his friends and colleagues thought that they were doing, and of the reasons for their success or failure.

[1] See for example, FRAZER 3.7, MURDOCK 3.18, R.A.I. 3.22.

We find ourselves at a time when a lot of attention was paid to primitive peoples. The ends of the earth were becoming not merely places of adventure and trade, but cruces of colonial administration. Moral and practical problems about the treatment of these peoples were in full view. The English movement for the abolition of slavery was young, and the *Société des amis des noirs* still younger. Frequent voyages of exploration, now no longer devoted to the physical task of making tracks on trackless seas, yielded more detailed reports of unfamiliar custom, strange physiognomy, and distant languages.

It was an impact that brought bewilderment, prejudice, and speculation. Prejudice, of course, had its familiar rôle of making an uncharted world manageable. Savages were inferior to Europeans; Savages were our equals and brothers; or Savages were our noble exemplar. Prejudices were trumpeted, with little attempt to assess the facts. Accepting one or the other prejudice justified the adoption of different sets of policies and views. To reject prejudice would have been to endorse empirical enquiries of unforseeable scope.

But speculation went further than prejudice. Was civilization the development of man's mind at the expense of his body? Did it bring evil and corruption where the savage led a happy and innocent life? What was the nature of savage society, religion, law, language, and how complex was it?

Such questions naturally and properly struck the European in face of the aboriginal. They were, too, a searching test of his own moral and intellectual qualities. Would he stand firm on prejudice, fly to speculation, or admit bewilderment and institute an arduous, dangerous, and interminable enquiry into the true answers to his questions? At length he took the right course, and social anthropology was born. But we return to our first question. When did this happen? Did not Degérando take one of the earliest steps in the present work?

It was already a sign of hope that painstaking collections of relevant observations began to be made. Curious compendia of shapes, habits and beliefs that might titillate a European reader, were giving way to scholarly and critical compilations of available material. It was the time of Court de Gébelin, Démeunier, and Pinkerton.[1] And a young French writer and pedagogue by the name of Louis-Francois Jauffret compiled, just after the turn of the century, a long series of memoirs destined to constitute an 'Histoire naturelle, morale et politique du genre humain', which was read in public, but never published.[2]

But compilations are not a substitute for fieldwork. The same Jauffret recognized this: it was to promote anthropological fieldwork of all kinds that he and a group of friends founded, at the end of 1799, the *Société des Observateurs de l'Homme*. The society attracted a formidable entourage of talented men – we shall soon see how much in earnest it was. At the same time, the project of empirical anthropological studies was new, and difficult to accept or practise. Difficult even to take seriously: a satire published in 1803 was entitled 'Report of a Meeting of the *Société des Observateurs de la Femme*'.[3]

Yet scepticism and satire must have an object. Indeed, it was just because enough people of importance did take 'the study of man' seriously, that it became a possible topic for satire.

Let us then look closely at the activities of the short-lived *Société des Observateurs de l'Homme*, and in particular at the story of Baudin's expedition to Australia, with which it had some association. We shall expect to find there the symptoms of, and the reasons for a sudden flowering, and a sudden withering, of social anthropology.

[1] See 2.8, 2.16, 2.44.
[2] See 1.3.
[3] See 2.18.

III

It is a story that begins and ends with the Consulate. We look to these five years, to the *Société des Observateurs de l'Homme*, and the Australian expedition, to what was done by Captain Baudin and the observers who accompanied him, and by Jauffret and Degérando, who stayed in France.

But first, we set the scene and introduce the chief characters.

Nicolas-Thomas Baudin was born in 1754 on the Ile de Rhe, off La Rochelle. He was an independent, resourceful, humane man, a skilled sailor, a tough captain. He won his name for botanical expeditions, especially for one made in the service of Francis I, on a vessel called *la Jardinière*, to China, Malaya, the Cape of Good Hope, and to the West Indies. On this occasion, specimens were left in Trinidad; and very shortly after his return to Europe, Baudin set sail again in *La Belle Angélique* to collect these specimens. He took with him three naturalists and a gardener. It was the autumn of 1796, and a difficult voyage was in store. First, the ship was shaken by severe storms, and was condemned at Tenerife. The French consul purchased the American brig *Fanny* to enable the expedition to continue, though with a reduced crew. Other tensions now played their part. At Trinidad, the safe-conduct issued for the crew of *La Belle Angélique* turned out to be almost useless for the crew of the *Fanny*, and Baudin was unable to collect his specimens. Politics frustrated the voyage. But Baudin sailed to the Virgin Islands where he took over a captured English ship, the *Triumph*, which he renamed *La Belle Angélique*. He then sailed, in some danger, to Puerto Rico, where he gathered a rich collection of specimens. But on his return to Europe, English patrols prevented his putting in at Le Havre; instead, he anchored at Fécamp, and the specimens were hurried by road to Paris, where they headed a procession of Bonaparte's Italian trophies. It was mid-1798. This eventful voyage rang bells. The naturalist Jussieu, director of the *Muséum d'Histoire Naturelle*, said of Baudin in a report to the Directory: 'Of all voyages, his is the one whose achievements in the sphere of natural history are most meritorious.' The *Moniteur français* announced 'the complete success of the voyage, which confirms the high opinion we already had of the commander's talent'. Baudin was well-placed to canvass for more work of the same kind.[1]

Indeed, by August 1798, two months after his arrival at Fécamp, Baudin seems already to have begun to press the project of a round-the-world voyage, destined especially for the West coast of South America, and for the 'terres nouvelles de la mer du sud'.[2] The Minister of Marine wrote on the matter to the *Muséum*, and received a favourable reply from Lacépède. In a few days, this letter was followed by a detailed report. South-West Australia was unexplored, and deserved special attention. Fleurieu would prepare a route. The *Muséum* would select scientific personnel: Baudin should be made captain, and select his crew for the expedition.

A day later, the Directory appointed Baudin as captain. The voyage was approved. But postponement followed. Two months later, in October, Baudin wrote to the Minister: since the round-the-world voyage had been indefinitely postponed, could he have another command? But the matter dragged on for more than a year. In early 1800, Baudin was still complaining of inactivity and unemployment.

In March of that year, he tried a new initiative in a letter to the *Institut national*. The expedition to the other side of the earth had been much delayed, but it

---

[1] On Baudin's life and reputation, see JOSÉ: 3.14.
[2] The account of the events leading to the approval of the Australian expedition is derived mainly from 1.11.MS.9439 folios 121 ff. For the commission's report, see 1.1, 1.8.

was a worthy project. 'History and political economy', wrote Baudin, 'need more extensive information about the peoples living in these climes, details about population, customs, forms of government, and about the kind of commercial relations that can be set up with them.' Let the *Institut* put the matter to the first consul, 'the hero who today holds in his hands the high destinies of France'.

The *Institut* responded by setting up a commission to consider the plan, consisting of Bougainville, Fleurieu, Duteil, Camus, Laplace, Lelièvre, Jussieu, Cuvier, Langlès, and Lacépède, a well-informed and efficient body.

In April 1800, the commission made its report. The scientific initiative had passed from the *Muséum* to the *Institut*. Indeed, both Jussieu and Lacépède were members of the commission, and there was no lessening of support for the expedition from botanists and naturalists. But the new move indicated an altogether broader set of scientific aims which the expedition might now be expected to fulfil, aims reflected not only in Baudin's letter to the *Institut*, but also in the very composition of their commission.

The report was altogether favourable; but it made one important modification to the plan. The expedition should not be conceived as a round-the-world voyage, but should have a specific object – Australia, especially the unexplored south coast.

The commission's report, and that of the Ministry of Marine were well received by Bonaparte. But it was two months before the official letter of approval was signed, in June.

The machine was now in motion, and in the next three months before Baudin's departure it worked at full stretch to foresee and provide everything that was needed.

But the needs of the expedition depended on its intended function. Till now, we have seen nothing but a group of men intent on a wide programme of scientific research. There was in fact much more. Take a plumb-line from the Egyptian expedition, which set off shortly before Baudin's arrival at Fécamp.

In this case, certainly, the first purposes were military, subserving possession, prestige and commerce. A new, rich and strategic French possession, seized in face of the ascendancy of the British navy would be a plum for the patriot. Moreover, the blockade was undermining French commerce overseas. The tremendous and increasing prosperity of Britain through trade was not merely an affront, but a hindrance to the struggling Republic. By 1799, the Directory admitted that not a single merchant ship was at sea under the French flag. And in the following year, France's total maritime trade (on her own and on neutral vessels) amounted to less than one five-hundredth of that of London alone. A French stronghold in the Middle East might help to correct this imbalance.[1]

Yet the most extraordinary feature of this expedition was surely its academic staff. It is difficult to think of a parallel to this alliance between military and scientific purpose. For soon after the arrival of the force in Egypt, the *Institut de Caire*, with four branches (mathematics, physics, political economy, literature and arts), an institution modelled on the recently created *Institut de France*, was set up in a palace, provided with 143 academics, and a printing press.

This academy certainly pursued its scientific aims, and the great work that issued, the *Description de l'Egypte*,[2] is a weighty and impressive piece of research. But it had other functions too.

Its first meeting was held at seven in the morning (a duly military hour) in August 1798 under the presidency of Bonaparte, who posed the following six questions for its study:

[1] See MAHAN: 3.16.
[2] JOMARD: 2.17.

1. How should ovens for making the army's bread be constructed?
2. What would be a suitable replacement for hops in the manufacture of beer?
3. How could Nile water be purified?
4. What were the relative advantages in Egypt of windmills and water-wheels?
5. How could gunpowder best be obtained there?
6. What was the state of Egyptian legislation, and how could it be improved?[1]

Science pursued the advancement of knowledge, but it might on the way cosset an army's belly. Further, those of the French nation who were little warmed by the coarse stuff of a victorious army, might take fire at the thought of France, a cultural harbinger. The notion became commonplace. In commending a later project, the *Moniteur français* for May 9th 1822 spoke of the Government's wish to have 'among the isles of Polynesia and Australia, some points where French vessels can transplant civilization and its benefits'.

Thus we see great complexity of purpose not only in the Egyptian expedition as a whole, but even in the presence of its scientific personnel. The point can be emphasized by considering the journey on which the Provisional Executive Council sent one Olivier in the first year of the Republic. He was to go to the Ottoman Empire, Egypt, and Persia; and his travels were supposed to promote the interests of commerce, agriculture, natural history, physics, geography, medicine, and political relations with the Turks.[2]

Now this brief consideration of the Egyptian expedition was intended to guide us setting out the various purposes envisaged for Baudin's venture.

In fact, there is evidence for a like range of aims in this case too.

Commerce for one. Of course, Baudin's voyage was not likely to serve any immediate commercial advan-

---

[1] See MAGASIN ENCYCLOPÉDIQUE: 2.22.
[2] ibid.

tage. But in the long run, much might be hoped for. We find these hopes expressed even in Degérando's memoir. And the great mariner Bougainville, a member of the commission of the *Institut national*, had made his own position clear more than thirty-five years before, writing in 1764 on the justification of voyages. 'The balance of commerce has become that of power. There is no commerce without navies, no navies without seafaring. France at present has not an amount of seafaring proportionate to the amount of commerce that she should have.'[1] Commerce had become a characteristic preoccupation of the time. It was not merely the great means of wealth, but even the great instrument for good. It was natural, then, that any seagoing venture should be considered as a possible means of advancing commerce.

But, as has been pointed out, commercial advantage could only be a long term hope. More immediate was the question of colonial possessions. The European powers were struggling, in the West Indies, and elsewhere. And of course, these possessions were not merely of strategic advantage: they had already proved to be one of the keys to the economic advancement of Britain. The value of British trade overseas increased by more than sixty-five per cent between 1792 and 1800.[2] The French authorities therefore began to consider the possible seizure of English colonial territories.

Accordingly, we find a number of what are best called 'spy-reports'. In early 1798, for example, one Lescallier, a former official in India now attached to the *Bureau des colonies*, presented to the Directory a memoir on India with recommendations for breaking the English stranglehold there.[3] He gave details of what alliances should be made and what other preparatory moves effected, and how best a large military expedition would succeed, and concluded by emphasizing the

---

[1] See BOUGAINVILLE, 1.13, folio 11.
[2] See MAHAN: 3.16.
[3] 1.12.

importance of this move as a preliminary to, or even a part of a direct attack on the English in Europe.

Similarly, a man called Marivault, French envoy to Holland, presented to the government in mid-1801 a memoir on the Cape of Good Hope.[1] He gave in much detail alternative plans for the capture of the Cape from the English, with a report on the method which they had themselves used to capture it, and a note of its importance. He recommended that it should subsequently be retained as a colony, or better, in the tradition of Adam Smith, given independence (referring of course to a European settlers' régime). However, the settlers had insufficient resources for defence and administration. They were inexperienced, uncivilized, and irresponsible. It would be better to institute an educational programme aimed at a subsequent independence. Marivault went on to list the necessary administrative staff for managing the Cape as a dominion, and concluded by stating what in his view the policy of that administration should be. First, it should in every way encourage free trade. It should promote agriculture, manufacture, mining, inner communications. It should permit free access to the territory. It should impose a small trading tax. So then would 'the inhabitants of the Cape become once more what their ancestors were formerly in the Low Countries, the factors of all peoples'. It is to be noted that although Marivault has much to say about the 'inhabitants of the Cape', his only mention of the real inhabitants is in a passage where he recommends that the army should include a section of Hottentots for policing the forests. To be expected. A military plan of this kind will have as its aim the advantage of France, primarily at the strategic, political and commercial levels. It is an aim that accords ill with any scientific or philanthropic interest in indigenous peoples, or with any concern for their rights.

We may expect then that if Baudin's expedition was

[1] 5.6.

to be the herald of an enlightened interest in aboriginal peoples which Degérando claimed it to be, espionage should not be among its functions. In fact, however, we shall have to uncover a spy on board. The Egyptian expedition will have proved a sadly reliable guide to the purpose of the expedition. And what of the attitudes of its personnel? Are we to find a guide to them too in the thoughts of Bonaparte's brother, sitting in his Egyptian tent, amid the *fellahin*, and writing 'Oh Jean-Jacques, you should have been here!'?

This is an underlying question of the whole introduction. The answer is ahead. At present, we are discussing the aims with which Baudin was sent on his expedition to Australia. And at present we have noted that military and commercial ones were not absent.

These apart, there was also, of course, concern for the interests of navigation. The waters to the South of Australia were completely uncharted, and an important function of the expebition was to provide satisfactory charts of this and other seas.

Again there was concern for national prestige. A patriot will welcome the discovery by French adventurers of unknown seas and lands. The knowledge that one's country is in anything a pioneer is a typical spring of patriotic feeling.

But we return, finally, to the scientific purposes with which we began. The expedition was provided with zoologists, botanists, geographers and mineralogists. But what of the study of man? It has already been noticed how Baudin, in his letter to the *Institut* of March 1800, spoke of the scientific interest of observations of aboriginal peoples. His was not a voice in the wilderness. In 1795, a French translation was published of John White's *Voyage to New South Wales*,[1] a work which had already begun to effect such observations. And in the same year, the great Orientalist Volney published in the *Magasin Encyclopédique* 135 'questions d'économie politique', on geography,

[1] 2.55.

climate, geology, products, population, agriculture, industry, commerce, government and administration.[1]

In the same year, Millin, editor of the *Magasin*, also like Volney a future member of the *Société des Observateurs de l'Homme*, published a fanciful book called 'Des variétés de l'espèce humaine, indiquées dans les poëmes d'Homère',[2] which was reviewed in his publication under the rubric 'Anthropologie'.[3]

IV

The study of man was in the air; but what it was to be, as this title shows, was uncertain. It is at this point that we introduce our second chief actor, Louis-François Jauffret. It was he, as has been noted, who took hold of this movement of interest, and tried to establish and develop it in founding the *Société des Observateurs de l'Homme*.

Louis-François was born in 1770, younger brother of André, future Bishop of Metz. After retiring to Orléans during the reign of terror, he returned to Paris and made a name for himself in the last decade of the century as a popular writer of works on education, and as the editor of the *Gazette des tribunaux*. It was at this time that he also became 'agent pour la partie scientifique' of the *Société de l'Afrique intérieure*, with what qualifications, it is difficult to say. The history and aims of the *Société de l'Afrique intérieure* are obscure. It was concerned, no doubt, with exploration, perhaps commerce. We know that Levaillant, well-known for his explorations in Africa, and his books about African birds, and another future member of the *Société des Observateurs de l'Homme*, was one of its directors. We know that the society had an agent for arms. These facts suggest commercial as well as scientific interest.

We left Baudin's expedition in preparation, in mid-

[1] 2.19.
[2] 2.41.
[3] 2.20.

1800. Now Jauffret is to found the *Société des Observateurs de l'Homme*, in December 1799. The story begins.

The society is founded by Jauffret and nine friends, of whom the most eminent is l'abbé Sicard, well known for his pioneering work in the education of deaf-mutes. Within three months, a distinguished membership marks the society, its first meeting is held, and its foundation is heralded in the *Magasin Encyclopédique*:[1] 'In taking the name *Société des Observateurs de l'Homme*, and the ancient motto Γνῶθι σεαυτόν, *Know thyself*, the society has devoted itself to the science of man, in his physical, moral, and intellectual existence; it has summoned to its observations the true friends of philosophy and moral being, the profound metaphysician, the practical doctor, the historian, the traveller, the student of the spirit of languages, the man who directs and protects the first developments of childhood. Thus man, followed and compared in the different scenes of life, will become the subject of research the more useful as it is free of any passion, prejudice, and above all of any love of system. The observers of man will work in good faith, and with the object of gathering more facts.'

It is well to read of good faith: but what kind of *facts* are we to expect of such a society? Among its early recruits mentioned in this article are Haller, a doctor; Degérando, a philosopher; Portalis, a lawyer and politician; Cuvier, a zoologist; Pinel, pioneer of the treatment of mental illness; Jussieu, a naturalist; Patrin, an explorer and mineralogist. The net is very wide. The society is devoted to aims so diffuse as to be necessarily superficial. The project of an anthropology is as yet no more than a possibility. Indeed, it has been noted how Millin, another member of the society, and editor of the *Magasin Encyclopédique*, thought that reading Homer was a satisfactory source of ethnological facts. This armchair approach, one that we took to

[1] 2.26.

be Degérando's merit to supplant, was indeed the commonplace of the period. John Richardson wrote *A Dissertation on the Languages, Literature, and Manners of Eastern Nations*, in which he commented: 'Travellers, in general, do not appear to have conceived a just idea of the situation of Women in many Eastern countries. They are for the most part considered by them as of small consequence in the state: they are represented as mere slaves to the passions of the stronger sex: etc. But an attention to the languages and customs of Asia, will give us reason to believe, that such indiscriminate observations are partial, superficial and inconclusive.' But his evidence for discounting travellers' reports is extraordinarily inappropriate: he cites etymologies, antique historians, historical anecdotes of the time of the prophet Muhammed; he uses European analogies. Indeed, the only obvious reference in the whole chapter to an anthropological fact properly so called is the following unattested footnote: 'The Tungos Tartar women consider it as a beauty to mark their face with black spots.'[1]

Such parallels should not encourage optimism about the *Société des Observateurs de l'Homme*. Indeed, this meeting, and the following two in June and July, show an ill-assorted set of topics. A deaf-mute describes his childhood; Patrin discourses on Siberia; the son of Portalis talks about the influence of great men on their age, a doctor discusses Rousseau's paradoxes of physical education, another doctor describes a case of amnesia, anecdotes are retailed about the Cantonese A-Sam, now in a hospital in Paris after being captured from an English ship bringing him and his family to Britain to develop commerce with China.

However, an impetus to serious and directed research had already been given, apparently at the first meeting. The commission set up by the *Institut* to enquire into Baudin's voyage, itself containing members of the society, already envisaged the possi-

[1] 2.49.

bility of anthropological observations. The explorer Levaillant brought the matter to Jauffret, who in his speech at the meeting spoke as follows: 'A single-minded devotion to developing the science of man will certainly bring a new age in the intellectual history of mankind... To achieve her aim, our society must not omit any opportunity of perfecting *anthropology*. There is one before us... An expedition round the world is about to take place under Captain Baudin. An eminent and worthy man, M. Levaillant, has given me the task of asking the society to provide sets of specific instructions on the research that should be carried out on men in the various countries to be visited by Baudin. The task is delegated to Hallé, Cuvier, Sicard, and Degérando.'[1]

So was the *Société des Observateurs de l'Homme* brought into the preparations for Baudin's voyage. Its commissioners produced two memoirs which may be regarded as the first serious statement of the aims and methods of anthropology.

The first was by Cuvier. Georges-Léopold-Chrétien-Frédéric-Dagebert Cuvier was born in 1769. He had been brought to Paris by Geoffroy de St. Hilaire, now at the *Institut de Caire*. Zoology was in a state of neglect, and he found eminent sponsors in Lamarck, Millin, Jussieu, and Lacépède. It was thanks to Lacépède that, in spite of his youth and lack of publications, he was elected to the *Institut de France* in 1795. His memoir for Baudin was concerned entirely with physical anthropology.

The other was the present work of Degérando. Joseph-Marie Degérando was born in 1772. His political activities in the '90s made it necessary to flee from France on two occasions. But he returned in time to win a prize from the *Institut* in 1799 for his philosophical discourse on *Signs*. Like Cuvier and Jauffret, he was among the young up and coming. Degérando was well aware of it: he liked others to be so too.

[1] See REBOUL: 3.21, p. 127.

There is an unsigned letter of his in the *Magasin Encyclopédique*, praising the memoir on signs, and citing Garat's opinion which would put him beside Locke and Condillac.[1] It is striking that he begins the present work by speaking of the 'age of egoism'.

However, it is his work on anthropology that chiefly concerns us, not his self-satisfaction, though this later will play its rôle. And it is to be noted here that his recommendations presuppose two requirements, first, that one or more people should be appointed to the expedition with the execution of Degérando's programme as their sole task (for the programme is certainly a full-time job); and secondly, that long stays should be made in particular places. His recommended observations would certainly take years rather than months, and in this he is making field-work a serious matter. But in this too, his seriousness may be questioned; for the proposed itinerary and duration of the voyage simply did not cater for such periods. Yet he does make his recommendations; is not altogether to be blamed if no one is ready to carry them out in the right way.

V

But will there be anyone to carry them out at all? The memoirs of Cuvier and Degérando are read at meetings of the *Société des Observateurs de l'Homme* in July and August. Degérando's work makes such an impression that it is subsequently decided to publish it. However, by the time of the reading the expedition's scientific personnel has already been chosen. The two vessels will take twenty-two men, astronomers, geographers, zoologists, botanists, mineralogists, artists, gardeners; but no anthropologists, or 'philosophical travellers'.

Was Degérando too late? It is at this point that Péron enters the story. François Péron was born in

[1] 2.21.

LOUIS FRANÇOIS JAUFFRET

F^ois PERON
(Voyageur),
Membre Correspondant de l'Institut.
Né à Cerilly (Dép.t de l'Allier) le 22 Août 1775.
Mort le 14 Décembre 1810.

1775. He joined the army in 1792, and lost his right eye in battle. In 1793, he was a Prussian prisoner of war. On his release two years later he returned to France. In 1797, he went to Paris, and began studies at the École de Médicine. He was a bright student. The expedition of Baudin caught his fancy, but could he gain a place when the scientific personnel had already been appointed? With the encouragement of Cuvier, he rushed out a brochure entitled *Observations sur l'anthropologie, ou l'histoire de l'homme, la nécessité de s'occuper de l'avancement de cette science et l'importance de l'admission sur la flotte du capitaine Baudin, d'un ou plusieurs naturalistes spécialement chargés des recherches à faire sur ce sujet*. In this work, he recognized the value of botany and zoology, but urged the importance of appointing 'some young doctors with the study of man as their specific task'. He speaks of a thorough study of the physical and moral being, the habits and customs, of the peoples to be visited.[1] His recommendations are close enough to those of Cuvier and Degérando. The projects of Jauffret, Lacépède, Cuvier and Degérando, are beginning to prosper. And Forfait, Minister of Marine, makes a special late appointment. Péron shall go with Baudin. It is odd that a report of the commission of the *Institut* gives his title as 'anatomiste des animaux'; but this is perhaps merely an administrative slip. The serious study of anthropology is about to begin.

However, the arrangements for the expedition have first to be completed, and this is far from a technicality. And amid all the enthusiasm, perhaps because of it, we see signs of danger.

Baudin, his officers and scientists, are overloaded with official instructions. There are the memoirs of Degérando and Cuvier. From Bernardin de St. Pierre, 'Expériences nautiques et observations diététiques proposées pour l'utilité de la navigation et la santé des marins'. Kéraudry, a doctor on the expedition, writes

---

[1] See the *éloge* of Péron in 2.43, vol. II, appendix.

sanitary instructions. Bauche (a nephew of Philippe) produces 'Observations astronomiques et géographiques pour servir au voyage du citoyen Baudin'. Copies of the instructions formerly given to La Pérouse are handed on. Fleurieu produces a detailed itinerary. But it is not simply a matter of volume. The Minister gives absurdly detailed orders for the expedition's time-table, in unknown seas.

More serious was the matter of crews. Baudin's previous voyages had been successfully conducted with four or five men of science. Now he was to have twenty-three. The captain thought this too many. In his view, their tasks did not warrant their number, the extra men would put a burden on provisions, and other personal and administrative difficulties would arise. Further, of the officers and the men of science on the two ships only four were men of experience, apart from the captain: Emanuel Hamelin, to be captain of the second ship; André Michaux, the botanist and explorer, now fifty-four; René Maugé, naturalist, and Anselme Riedlé, gardener, both veterans of Baudin's previous expedition. The rest were mainly young men of promise, or with influential connections. The average age of those whose age can be determined was twenty-seven, and many were not long in their twenties.

Baudin had a heavy task. On the one hand a programme of research that was too demanding, on the other, a body of inexperienced men to mould to an arduous and difficult voyage. But these signs of danger were lost in the general enthusiasm, except to the captain himself. The highest hopes were entertained.

Perhaps the most eloquent document to the spirit in which the expedition set out is to be found in the report of a farewell dinner given by the *Société de l'Afrique Intérieure* in Baudin's honour, with members of the *Société des Observateurs de l'Homme* and of the *Institut* as guests. The dinner was held in August, before Baudin left Paris to make his final preparations.

We read in the *Magasin Encyclopédique*:[1] 'It can be confidently stated that it is long since we have witnessed an assembly so remarkable in its object, and so interesting in the persons of whom it was composed. The presence of several famous travellers, of the venerable Bougainville, of Baudin, to whom Bougainville is entrusting his son, and who is to follow his steps; of Levaillant, who is to return to Africa and spend the rest of his life there; of Patrin, who travelled for ten years in the icy wastes of Siberia; the aspect of men like Jussieu, Fourcroy, Hallé, Pinel, Portalis, Thouin, and of a great many other men of learning, electrified and melted every heart. The following toasts were delivered.

LEVAILLANT, *one of the directors of the Society*: To the vessels *le Naturaliste* and *le Géographe*, under the command of Captain Baudin. May they travel without danger to the ends of the earth!

BAUDIN: To Bonaparte, first consul of the French Republic, protector of the arts and sciences. To the hope that I may once more, returning from my expedition, be in the same room with the same persons.

MEIFREDY, *son of Louis, one of the directors*: To the prosperity of commerce. May all those who love our land fasten their attention on this most important part of public prosperity!

JUSSIEU: To the progress of the physical and natural sciences, to which the voyages of Baudin and Levaillant will make a valuable contribution; and above all to citizens Maugé and Riedlé, who accompanied Captain Baudin on his expedition to the West Indies, and who would follow him to the end of the world; for one of them being struck through excessive fatigue with a very serious illness, it was the will of Captain Baudin himself to tend the sick bed.

DARQUIER, *agent of armaments of the society*: To the amelioration of the lot of the Savages. May their

[1] 2.28.

civilization result from the visit which the French are about to make them!

JAUFFRET: To the progress of anthropology. May the *Société des Observateurs de l'Homme* be one day honoured by the useful researches of its illustrious corresponding members!

FOURCROY: To the mariner Bougainville. May his son, following his footsteps, be, like him, the servant of science and humanity!

DEMAIMIEUX: To the return of Dolomieu, an inmate of this house.

BOUGAINVILLE: To the return of Captain Baudin and of the observers taking part in his expedition.

HALLÉ: To those who are co-operating in Baudin's voyage.

MILLIN: To the islanders who will be able to value the good works of the intrepid mariners, who are going, at the peril of their life, to bring them civilization, useful arts, and the love of humanity.

BISSY, *astronomer of the expedition*: To the *Institut national*.

LEBLOND: To the *Institut national* and to all the learned societies of Europe. May the union of their enlightenment and of their labours efface to the last traces all political dissension

Citizen Brielle sang very tastefully several pieces appropriate to the occasion.

Citizens Baillot, Tariot and Baudiot performed a trio with the greatest accomplishment.

Several musicians of the 'garde des consuls' contributed to the brilliance of the festivities.

Citizen Jauffret, junior, sketched during the dinner a portrait of Captain Baudin, and the whole company applauded the resemblance.

Elegant turns and high expectations. And an anomaly to mark our distance from reality, as the agent for armaments for the *Société de l'Afrique Intérieure* raises his glass to the amelioration of the lot of the savages.

VI

The expedition was late setting off,[1] mainly because of delays in the arrival of supplies; and there was a presage of friction in the behaviour of J.-G. Milbert, a man of thirty-four, one of the artists appointed to the expedition. Baudin wrote to Jussieu just before his departure: 'Everyone is here, but everyone is not equally happy. Each [of the *savants*] wanted a cabin, but this wasn't possible. Citizen Milbert, though he has one, constantly threatens to return to Paris; I think that he'd only like a pretext to set out. Will he be a pest? I don't know.'

For all these omens, the early part of the voyage went perfectly. Sent on their way with warm wishes from the British frigate which inspected their passport on the first day, the two vessels made an excellent passage to Tenerife. The scientific personnel suffered somewhat from sea-sickness. Otherwise, they all behaved very well. Perhaps, comments Baudin in a letter from Tenerife, they showed rather too much enthusiasm, and rather too little reflectiveness. The astronomers, Bissy and Bernier, and the mineralogist, de Puche, were a little weak. But Péron was working well, and Milbert had belied his earlier temperament. The zoologists Maugé and Lharidon were hard at work, and already in a few days at Tenerife had collected a large quantity of specimens.

With good presages, then, the two vessels, *le Géographe* under Baudin and *le Naturaliste*, under Emanuel Hamelin, soon set sail on the long haul to Mauritius.

In the first weeks, two amusing incidents are recorded in Baudin's journal. The first 'though it was very disagreeable for Péron provided great amusement to his fellow scientists and most of the officers who saw it. At midday, Péron was in the port scuppers making observations with a thermometer, when he was

---

[1] For the following account of the expedition, see 1.9, 1.10, 1.11; 2.2, 2.34, 2.43; 3.3, 3.4, 3.6, 3.8, 3.9, 3.14, 3.24. A few detailed references are given in the course of the account.

drenched by a wave. He came to no harm, but thought himself hopelessly drowned; and when the water had drained out of the scuppers, he found it amazing not only that he was alive, but also in the same place, for he thought he'd been carried out to sea!' Ten days later, Baudin was walking on the quarter-deck; 'Péron rushed up, dripping with blood, and complaining that Lharidon had *stolen the heart of the shark*. The duty officer did his best not to laugh at a complaint which Doctor Péron made so serious. To console him, I promised that the very next shark would be all his own.'

While these diversions were taking place, however, a serious problem was making itself felt. The expedition was already behind time; and it was becoming unavoidably obvious that *le Naturaliste* was a slow vessel. The expedition's time-table was threatened. In an attempt to compensate for this, Baudin diverged from the official course. But it was a vain attempt, for the currents and winds were wrong. Mauritius was reached in mid-March 1801, two months after the date laid down, and a month after the latest date stated for departure from the island.

But after the long stage from Tenerife, a rest for the men was essential. Moreover, their health, though till now unmarred, required care. Many provisions were needed.

Tempers had become short too, towards the end of the long spell at sea. But right conduct and discipline had to be maintained. As Mauritius was approached, Baudin called together the scientists and officers, and reproached them with their conduct, particularly their quarrelsomeness. If they did not behave better, they would be put ashore.

But worse problems than this were in store. Since the Revolution, Mauritius had broken from direct French control, primarily because of the decree of 1794 abolishing slavery in French colonies. In 1796, General Magallon was sent with a naval division and 1,200 troops. Part of his task was to re-establish French authority. But this failed. The settlers announced their complete dependence on the slave economy. Slavery could not be abolished. However, Magallon remained on the island. Soon before Baudin arrived, indeed, he had succeeded Malartic, who died in July 1800. Here was a refractory colony, suspicious of visitors from the motherland.

When Baudin arrived, he was not admitted to port before he had, with some difficulty, persuaded the régime that there was no French official aboard with the task of putting into effect the decree against slavery. It was a poor beginning, and troubles did not cease. Provisions were refused by the régime. As a result, men fell ill who would otherwise have been soon in full health, given proper food. The hospitals were put to work. Moreover, all Baudin's representations failed to extract the provisions he needed from the administration. It was only when he found foreign traders in Mauritius prepared to accept his signature as a guarantee of payment by the French government that he was able to obtain the provisions indispensable to the continuation of the expedition.

Moreover, the comforts of the island after a long period at sea were undermining the expedition's morale. Many stayed ashore merely through the pretence of illness. And while some continued the work of gathering fauna and flora, most entertained themselves in the town. Such difficulties are inevitable, wrote Baudin, in a letter to Jussieu, when men are appointed 'who are too young to be able to appreciate the loss of time'. By the time Baudin left, ten of the scientific personnel of the expedition had abandoned it, through sickness real or feigned, through a dislike of the hardships of sea voyages, or through a dislike of Baudin himself, uncompromising captain.

Baudin reported in the same letter that three found jobs teaching mathematics and drawing in the schools of the island, and one got married. 'I am unaware of the high destiny of the others', he commented wryly.

We know, however, the destiny of one, at least. J.-B.-G.-M. Bory de St. Vincent, one of the four zoologists, a young man of only twenty, returned to France and cashed in on the interest in the expedition by composing a government-sponsored account of the first part of the voyage,[1] in which he falsely described himself as 'chief naturalist', and which consisted in large part of the libel of his former commander.

Not all those who left were worthless. André Michaux, the famous naturalist already mentioned, had, before embarking, specifically reserved the right to leave the expedition. And now he decided to stay in Mauritius. Man of an independent mind: he soon went to Madagascar, where he pursued his botanical researches, and, as he had formerly done in so many parts of the world, founded a nursery. He died there a year later. None of Baudin's arguments about his obligations to the government and its expedition had had any effect.

On the whole, however, Baudin was not concerned about the exodus of men (which was not confined to the scientists of the expedition). Some had been expected to leave, like the Cantonese A-Sam who was to be taken thus far by Baudin on his long journey home. And the rest were in any case the least worthy and valuable members. In any case, Baudin had already complained about being overstaffed.

Nevertheless, this partial collapse was a bad symptom of the state of the venture, and an ill omen for its conclusion. It has already been noticed too, that Baudin was badly behind schedule. His departure in late April was two months late. The advent of winter in the southern seas was too close.

The official plan had been that Tasmania should be reached by March 1801, by sailing on the high seas direct from Mauritius. The unknown southern coast of Australia was then to be surveyed in detail from

[1] 2.2.

east to west, and from June to August the expedition would winter in the South-west. The western coast would then be explored, and the north-western extremity of the continent reached by October. From there, still in October, course would be set north-east to the island of Timor, where the expedition would stay for two months, leaving in December for Waigeo, a small island to the north-west of New Guinea. New Guinea would be briefly explored. From April to July 1802 a detailed survey of the Gulf of Carpentaria. Then the expedition was to return to Mauritius.

However, the late departure from Mauritius threw out the whole plan. It would not now be possible to reach Tasmania in time to survey the south coast and reach south-west Australia by June. In fact, it was already May 27th when Cape Leeuwin was first sighted. Accordingly Baudin decided to pick up the official time-table, making observations in the West forthwith, and to return later for a survey of the Southern coast.

The expedition remained for more than two months in the area south of Perth, near what are still called 'Cape Naturaliste', and 'Géographe Bay'. The business of making observations, drawing maps, collecting specimens, goes on apace.

And here at last is the test for which we have been waiting – the opportunity for the practice of anthropology. Would Péron carry out his task?

When compared with a theoretical promise, what was actually done (as recorded in Péron's official account) was pitiful.

On one occasion Péron pursues some timid natives of the place, without success. He gives an account especially concerned with the analysis of his own emotions. On another, he found some kind of ceremonial grove (a 'bora ground'). After giving a description of it, he yields himself to cultivated and well-phrased speculation: 'New Egyptians, perhaps, like the ancient inhabitants of the Nile, (these peoples) will have hallowed . . . the river which nourishes them. . . . Perhaps, at solemn times, they come to its bank to pay a tribute of homage and gratitude.' We are invited to turn our minds to runes, to Mexican hieroglyphs, to ceremonial grounds of Ceylon and South Africa. Péron sits, letting his mind wander. Then he moves away again 'after giving to the examination of this grove all the attention that it was worth'.[1]

Encounters with the savages are mentioned. One of the officers met an old man and a pregnant woman, and saw some huts. 'I thought,' wrote Péron, 'that there could be no worse condition of mankind. But I was wrong. We were far from having seen, in the matter of dwelling places or any other details of physical and social existence, the ultimate of ignorance and misery. . . .'[2] And if we wonder *what* details, it is vain to look in Péron's record.

On another occasion, the mineralogist de Puche and some colleagues met a crowd of aborigines. They tried to make contact, but without success. Thinking themselves threatened by assegais, they took the obvious step of laying down their guns and waving white handkerchiefs! But the aborigines didn't get the point, and went away. Péron concludes confidently that the savages of this area flee from or repel strangers.[3] The perceptive words of Degérando on this matter are quite forgotton.

Péron so far shows himself an entirely superficial observer. The idea of a serious empirical study of anthropology has not taken root in him at all. His performance is markedly inferior to that of many travellers of the period without scientific pretensions.

However, Péron was a young man, and this his first encounter: the subjects perhaps were particularly difficult. Indeed, his performance improved considerably on the island of Timor.

[1] 2.43, vol. I, pp. 76–7.
[2] ibid., p. 82.
[3] ibid., pp. 84–90.

Baudin reached the island on August 21st and stayed for 84 days. During that time, Péron was hard at work. 'In Timor', he wrote, 'are three distinct races of men, who, placed together on these shores since a period whose date is lost in the night of time, still are plain to the observer, with all the original characteristics of the ancient people to which each belongs. To the first of these races belong the indigenous inhabitants pushed back into the interior, still foreign to practically any social institution, armed still with the bow and arrow and club of *Camouny*, sworn enemies of the Malays, swift in running, hidden away in the hollows of rocks or the depths of forests, living only on fruit and game, always under arms, always at war, whether between themselves or with the Malays, fierce in their tastes, in all their cannibal habits, it is said, and possessing all the characteristics of the Negro race, properly so called, short, woolly and fuzzy hair, black colour etc. To the second class of inhabitants of Timor belong the *Malays*, with long hair, and the colour of red leather. Issue of those fierce dwellers in Malaya, ancient conquerors of the great archipelago of Asia, the men of this race still preserve the independent, audacious and proud character which distinguished their ancestors. Beside these valorous peoples, the Chinese multiply. For centuries, they have been established on most of the islands of the archipelago, skilful merchants, tireless second-hand dealers, cowardly and weak men who could nowhere obtain authority, or deserve it.'[1]

This is poor enough stuff: but it shows more industry. Much of it indeed, might have been gathered from casual talk. But yet Péron did engage in some real field-work. He met some hospitable Malays in the interior. 'They will remember us', he wrote. 'The French name will long be dear to them.' Their first words were 'Dondon, dondon, bâé oran di France' ('Sit down, sit down, good men of France'). Soon,

[1] ibid., p. 144 ff.

they came out with 'Oran Ingress, oran bounou' ('Englishmen, murderous men'), and repeated bitterly 'Oran djâhăt' ('wicked men'). They mimed massacre, and expressed in every way their feelings of horror and vengeance towards the English. After this, Péron's host had his five wives enter. They were beautiful and charming.[1]

On a later occasion, a visit was made to the king of the island of Savu. The king's companions stole most of the possessions of their French guests. Péron writes: 'Stealing is a sort of passion in the Malays, and their skill in it is such, that they made fools of us all. They share this vice with all savage people or people of little civilization; this proves, we may comment in passing, that legislators have been right to consecrate the right of property as the foundation of social institutions.'[2]

It can hardly be said, with all this, that anthropology is prospering, or even appearing. Péron may be making observations in the field, but his capacity for close or systematic study, and for reasoned statement and conclusion can only be described as minimal.

He did, however, have one important capacity (however insufficient on its own) – that of taking an interest in and befriending particular people. 'Among the individuals whom I had occasion to get to know with any intimacy during our stay at Timor was a respectable old man whose noble and frank face caught my interest more each day. He had observed my taste for the productions of the sea coast, and often came to offer me the tribute of his fishing and of his searching: the generous way in which I was pleased to express my gratitude for his kindly offices had succeeded in gaining me the good wishes of the good old man; I was his 'sobat ati' ('his bosom friend'). He had several times invited me, in the most pressing way, to go to visit his house, though my work had not yet allowed me to satisfy his wishes in this respect. . . . But

[1] ibid.
[2] ibid., p. 150.

on September 4th, I went with de Puche and Bernier, guided by one of his sons. . . . He had a humble hut, like those of the poorest Malays of this region. The simplicity of this sort of dwelling seemed to add a fresh charm to the delightful countryside which surrounded it. . . . The old man . . . was sitting at the entrance to his hut, busy playing the *Sasounou*; a younger son than the one who had brought us accompanied him on the strange flute of these shores; his wife, some paces from him, was spinning the braid of rushes which these peoples use to weave their loincloths, and his daughter, who seemed only twelve or thirteen, was preparing some little rice cakes which she had to take the following day to sell at the bazaar.'[1]

Occasional passages like this in his official account of the expedition show in Péron the capacity for a form of encounter exceedingly valuable to the anthropologist. But, as can be seen, he treated such an encounter as a luxury that took him away from his real work. It is clear that the memoir 'Sur l'anthropologie' which gained him his place on the expedition, represented little of what he really believed or understood.

Timor was the scene of other disenchantments. The health of the crew suffered severely. Many, including the captain, were badly hit by dysentery. In October, Anselme Riedlé, the industrious chief gardener, old friend and colleague of Baudin, died. He was buried in the same grave as David Nelson – a botanist who had died at his arrival on Timor ten years earlier after completing the long and remarkable voyage in an open boat with Lieutenant William Bligh, after the Bounty mutiny. Three members of Baudin's crew perished at the same time.

But it was time to return south, and make the survey of the south coast of Australia. Ill health continued to mar the voyage. At sea died Antoine Sautier, assistant gardener, Stanislas le Villain, naturalist, and five more members of Baudin's crew. During the same period,

[1] ibid., p. 154 ff.

Hamelin, on *le Naturaliste*, lost seven men. It was a gloomy time between the departure from Timor in November 1801 and the arrival in Tasmanian waters in January 1802. And now, René Maugé, the chief zoologist of the expedition, after a brief recovery from illness, perished in his turn on Maria Island, a small island to the south-east of Tasmania. In his journal for February 20th, Baudin recorded the dying words of Maugé: 'I am dying because I was too much attached to you, and therefore scorned the advice given me by friends. At least remember me, and thus repay the sacrifice I made for you.' Baudin was deeply moved by the deaths of Riedlé and Maugé. 'So they perished,' he wrote, 'the only true friends I had on board.'

But a three-month stay in Tasmanian waters was the opportunity for more observations by Péron. We have been led to expect little, and little we find. Triebel's comment, that Péron's work was a 'monument of careful and truthful observation' of the savages of Tasmania, is an extraordinary falsehood.[1]

In fact, we find a straight traveller's account, like those from Péron that have already been instanced, but somewhat more copious. The faults are still there: and they are indeed those very faults which Degérando had so clearly exposed. There is in fact no sign of the 'philosophical traveller', at least in the activities of François Péron. Captain Baudin himself was much nearer to understanding what ought and ought not to be done, though he was a man with no academic pretensions.

In a letter to Jussieu, he devoted substantial passages to accounts of 'les naturels' in Tasmania, especially on Bruni island. In these passages he remarks on the difficulty of determining the character of the savages from their behaviour towards him – a healthy uncertainty which the speculative enthusiasm of Péron never permitted. Baudin notes, in detail, their physical appearance, their reaction to various sorts of presents,

[1] 3.24.

their unfamiliarity with the use of nets for fishing, their disdain of a cauldron, their love of bottles, their established fear of firearms, their use of tattooing, their custom that women do the work (like gathering seafood), their canoes and the manner of manufacturing them, their nudity, their custom of habitually holding the foreskin between finger and thumb, making it very long, their disdain for axes, knives, scissors and hammers, their amazement at the sight of goats and a sheep, which they attempted to engage in conversation. Drawings were made of the savages' huts and utensils. Baudin's account, as can be seen, is reasonably detailed and properly guarded. He permits himself only one speculation: 'I think that the use of fire is quite unknown to them, not only because of their disdain for the tools which we wanted to give them, but also because of their indifference and lack of attention on seeing us make use of it.' And this is carefully marked as a speculation. The observers of the expedition were less cautious. Baudin wrote: 'One of our *savants* claims that (the savages) eat a sort of bracken with a farinaceous root. He even adds that he has incontestable proof that in times of scarcity they eat grass. Since the proof of his view lies in some dried-up excrement, it can be judged how well founded this conjecture is.' And again: 'People have believed themselves to have noticed (the savages) looking frequently at the sun, and have readily persuaded themselves that this must be their divinity. But I have seen nothing of the kind, and believe them as lacking in ideas of this kind as they are in industry for their own survival.'

However, Baudin's severity about speculations of this kind does not reach the point of arrogance. He concludes his remarks as follows: 'I shall say no more about the Tasmanian natives, leaving this to our *savants*, who have perhaps made a better study of them than I.'

Yet he was not confident about their capacity. He wrote in the same letter: 'Since I have often criticized their conduct, their method of research, and their reasoning, since I have frequently urged them to follow the example of Maugé and Riedlé, whom they considered below them, and spend more time working, and less speculating, they haven't passed on the results of their scientific work to me for a long time. Perhaps they're afraid of the criticism of a man who is not educated in the way that they are, and who has more than once shown disapproval of schematic descriptions and wild conjectures; but, more likely, they thought that I could arrogate the credit which they take for the least object that their fertile imagination distorts on sight as in description. In any case, I nonetheless hope that they have fulfilled the intentions of the government, and the expectations of the truly learned men who judged them to be of use for this enterprise, and that we finish our task before the fear of death takes most of them to a premature grave.'

Before leaving Tasmania, the expedition spent some time on Maria Island, the scene of the death of Maugé. Baudin relates a striking incident. Some members of the crew were cutting firewood. Armed savages approached, and a carpenter of *le Naturaliste* was cut off. He was taken away, and stripped naked by the savages, who made a scrupulous examination of his whole body, after which he was permitted to dress, and go away with his axe, having suffered no harm. Baudin remarks: 'It would perhaps be just as interesting for the study of man to know what the thoughts of the carpenter were in these circumstances, as to know the reasons for the curiosity of the savages.'

But Péron was not much interested in this. He found a burial ground, and it provided material for the kind of high speculations which he had indulged earlier at the bora ground near Géographe Bay. Baudin's strictures on speculation were to no effect. How vulgar and uncultivated to suggest the laborious and pedestrian task of uncovering the facts about such phenomena!

However, there was little opportunity for further anthropological research or speculation in Tasmania: the expedition soon set out to conduct at last its survey of the unknown southern coast of Australia.

A detailed account would tell of the loss of the geographer Boulanger and seven sailors in a long-boat, of the separation of *le Naturaliste* and *le Géographe*, of the unexpected meeting with Matthew Flinders in what is still called 'Encounter Bay'. Flinders, in his ship *The Investigator*, had set off from Europe eight months after Baudin, and was engaged in a similar task. At the time of the meeting, Flinders had already surveyed a substantial part of the unknown coast. Baudin warned the English captain of some dangerous rocks, which Flinders subsequently named after him. Flinders gave Baudin some charts, and suggested that he should return to Port Jackson (Sydney) after completing his own survey.

But by the time Baudin had reached the Isles of St. Francis, winter was approaching, supplies of water and wood were very short, and scurvy attacked the crew so badly that there were only twelve sailors fit for work. Thus, in early May 1802, the captain was forced to turn back from his survey, and make for Sydney.

At the end of June, the port was reached, and there was good news to compensate for difficulty and disease. Boulanger and the men in the long boat had been picked up by an English ship; and *le Naturaliste* after a twenty-day stay at Sydney had set sail for France. Soon, the second ship returned. Wind had prevented Hamelin doubling Cape Leeuwin for Mauritius.

So was the expedition reunited. King, the English governor of Port Jackson, received it well. The sick were tended in hospital, supplies were provided, and researches in the territory by the French naturalists were encouraged. The indigenous population had largely retreated to the interior, and it was noticeable that they were quicker at learning English than the English at learning their tongue. Here was another opportunity for Péron to show his mettle. The expedition stayed for six months in the area, yet the observations which issued are of no account. In fact, his main anthropological activity was to cavort with an instrument specially made for the expedition by one Requier, and called a 'dynamometer'. It was a device intended to measure physical strength. The question to be answered was 'Does civilization vary inversely with strength?' Péron did have the sense to remark that the question cannot be resolved in general, but he measured the strength of eighty-five savages of Timor, Tasmania, and the Australian continent, and used French and English subjects as a control group. And in spite of his earlier warnings, he goes on to conclude that the claim that civilization varies inversely with strength is shown by his measurements to be false. The validity, as well as the purpose, of the experiment might be questioned. Did the aborigines know what they were supposed to be doing with this machine? The final absurdity is the admission in Péron's account that he had misused the dynamometer by reading the wrong scale.[1] But the taking of such measurements was a minor task, and as has already been remarked, Péron's research in Sydney was negligible. In fact, as we shall later discover, he was otherwise occupied. He was a spy.

Of course, Baudin, good patriot, was not insensible to political issues. He wrote to Jussieu: 'If the English take possession of Tasmania, it will truly be a loss for France; for an establishment to the South of Tasmania could only have great commercial advantage, and seems politically necessary.'[2] He commented that the whale trade with China was enormous, and that there was evidence that the English did not want the French to cut in on it. But we have no evidence that the

---

[1] ibid., p. 476; vol. II, p. 460 ff.
[2] I.10.

French government had given Baudin any political brief. And moreover, commerce and politics are not the only questions that arise about a project of colonization. When King wrote to him asking about French territorial ambitions, Baudin replied: 'I have never been able to conceive that Europeans have either justice or equity on their side when in the name of their governments they annex lands newly found by them but already inhabited by men who do not always deserve the name of "savage" or "cannibal".... I have no knowledge of any pretensions the French government may have to Van Diemen's Land, nor of its designs for the future; but I think its title no better grounded than yours.'[1] We may ask which of the two letters represents Baudin's real view, so far as they are at odds; but even were we to take his moral objections in the letter to King as humbug, it is remarkable enough that he could have produced the idea at all at that time. Adam Smith's passing remark to the same effect seems to have had little influence.[2] Thus, the extraordinary unorthodoxy of Baudin's protest makes it difficult to take it as a piece of flannelling.

A picture of Baudin emerges as a humane, level-headed, hard-working man, capable of treating the most alien men as fellow beings. We might be led to say: here could have been the anthropologist of the expedition. But he was captain, and had other concerns.

And those concerns were pressing at the time. It was late 1802, the date laid down for the arrival of the expedition at Mauritius on the return voyage. The survey of Australia's southern coast was yet incomplete, and New Guinea and the Gulf of Carpentaria unvisited. Moreover, crews had been seriously reduced by the ravages of scurvy and dysentery. The slow and deep-draught *Naturaliste* was a hindrance to the work of surveying. And there were forty thousand specimens

[1] 2.5.
[2] 2.52, Book IV, chapter VII.

of all kinds of flora and fauna, alive and dead, whose survival would be threatened by the continuation of the expedition.

Baudin therefore decided to send *le Naturaliste* back to France. This much less trying voyage could be carried out with a smaller crew than would be needed for further exploration. The less satisfactory men could be sent back. The preservation of the specimens would be better served, and the work of surveying made easier.

The command of the voyage was left to Hamelin: though Baudin regretted parting with him, there was no other suitable officer. With him went all the midshipmen but two, one who had been made up to the rank by Baudin on the voyage, having been too young at the outset, and the other – the future admiral, Charles Baudin, unrelated to Nicolas. Seeing the others go, the captain commented on their confidence that on their return, name or patronage would at once make them first officers. He wrote to Jussieu that in fact none of them had been at all useful or efficient. On the contrary, they had been insolent, overbearing, and reluctant to learn. Hamelin's crew, on the other hand, though it was to comprise the least healthy, had acquitted itself well.

The second measure that Baudin took for the continuance of the expedition was to buy a small schooner of thirty tons, which he named the *Casuarina*, after the wood of which it was made. The command was given to Louis Freycinet, the younger of two brothers who were officers with the expedition (he was now twenty-three), and a man who was to lead, in 1817, another expedition of research to Australia.

But now, in December 1802, the three ships set out, *le Naturaliste* bound for France, and the other two in pursuit of their task.

There is little more to report that has any bearing on the practice of anthropology. The survey of the southern coast of Australia was completed, and

Baudin made for Timor, which was reached in May 1803. New Guinea and the Gulf of Carpentaria remained untouched.

For at Timor once more illness struck. The expedition arrived in May. In June, died P.-F. Bernier, a young astronomer of promise who had been only twenty on joining the expedition. And Leschenault de la Tour, the naturalist, badly struck by disease, remained in Timor, later to continue further explorations in the region. In fact, the whole expedition was affected; and Baudin himself suffered again from seriously impaired health. Supplies were difficult to come by, and the expedition was already a year behind schedule. Baudin decided that he could do no other than curtail the planned route, and sail straight for Mauritius.

The colony was reached in August. It was the end of the expedition; and that end was marked by the death of its captain. Admiral Baudin, later recalling the expedition, spoke in general of its difficulties. The personnel, he said, was too numerous, too young, and too inexperienced. The midshipmen were a scatter-brained lot. And of the death of the captain on September 16th 1803, he wrote: 'His obsequies were nothing less than melancholy: he was universally detested. He had shown great will-power in his last days. He had collected in a bottle of spirits of wine his lungs, which he had vomited out in unparalleled suffering, and he showed them to everyone who came to visit him. "Are the lungs necessary to life?" he would say. "You can see that I have no more, and yet I'm still alive." '[1]

A grim and apt epilogue to an expedition of great achievements, and great failures.

VII

The failure which most concerns us, however, is the

[1] Cited by Bouvier, 3.3.

miscarriage suffered by a newly conceived science. François Péron had been a disappointing choice for anthropologist. But he was still alive, and still capable of making others think well of him, by his personal charm, or by his well-contrived lies. And there were other means still.

In 1802, Charles-Matthieu-Isidore, Comte Decaen, the thirty-three-year-old general, had been appointed 'capitaine générale des possessions françaises à l'est du Cap de Bonne-Espérance'. He left Paris in March 1803, hot for the Indian struggle, but in view of the imminent war with England was ordered to retire to Mauritius. An active soldier, concerned more with strategy than research. In December 1803, two months after Baudin's death, Péron, who was still on the island, wrote a long report to Governor Decaen, noting the dangers of the English establishment at Sydney.[1] 'Always alive to what might humiliate the eternal rival of our nation,' he wrote, 'the first consul, immediately after the revolution of 18 brumaire, decided on our expedition. Its real and official purpose was too important to do anything but conceal it from all the peoples of Europe, and particularly from the Cabinet of St. James; we had to obtain universal agreement, and for that purpose, it was essential to appear quite unconcerned with political matters, and to concern ourselves only with collections in the field of natural history. . . . But it was far from our real object to confine ourselves to this kind of work, and if I had time, it would be very easy, citizen Captain-General, to show you that all our research in natural history, trumpeted with such ostentation by the government, was throughout only the pretext for its venture, was throughout to ensure its most general and complete success. Thus this expedition, so much criticized by small minds, so much neglected by the former administrators of this colony, was yet in its principle, in its object, in its organization, one of those

[1] See 1.6, MS. 5651.7.

brilliant conceptions which are to the eternal glory of our present government. Why should it be that after doing so much for what its designs required, it entrusted their execution to a man the least suited in every possible way to carry them through to their conclusion? . . . You asked me, General, to convey to you the information I was able to gather on the colony of Port Jackson.' Péron gives in great detail an account of the colony at Sydney. He concludes his report as follows: 'I must confine myself to declaring that I share with all those of my colleagues who have particularly concerned themselves with the organization of this colony, the opinion that it should be destroyed as soon as possible. . . . Today, we could do so easily; in twenty-five years, it would no longer be possible.'

So we learn why Péron virtually executed no research during the long stay at Sydney. His enquiries had another object. He was busy spying.

But what are we to make of Péron's claim that the real purposes of the expedition were strategic?

It is certainly true that Bonaparte had ambitions for French colonial expansion in the East. Moreover, there are some minor indications of duplicity in the case of Baudin's expedition. The British passport, for example, was issued for a round-the-world voyage, though it had long been decided that the specific object of the voyage was to be the exploration of Australia. And we have already noticed an anomaly in Péron's title: he applied to join the expedition for the study of primitive peoples, but he was called 'anatomiste des animaux'. Again, we have observed that Forfait, the Minister of Marine, agreed to appoint him at the last minute. Could he have been given a hidden brief, to make the strategic judgments and observations which were the real purpose of the expedition?

It is a far-fetched speculation. A young extroverted student is the last person to be entrusted with such a task. Moreover, as a master-plan of colonial strategy, the expedition was a joke. Of course, the results of the venture would not be irrelevant to colonial ambitions, and it well fitted Bonaparte's interest in such schemes. It has already been remarked that the expedition was not without strategic aims of the most general kind.

But Péron's protestations to Decaen are risible. He was certainly a self-appointed spy, a self-hailed executive of a non-existent project. He was, in fact, ready to establish his position by taking whatever seemed likely to be the most popular line. Four years later, he was writing: 'On the far shores that we were to visit, dwelt peoples interesting to know; the first consul wished that, representatives of Europe to these forgotten men, we should appear among them as friends and benefactors.'[1]

But whatever Péron's status, and whatever his variability, the report to Decaen is an apt testimony to his fitness for the science he professed.

Yet this was the failure of one man; and till now, we have seen it as a failure of character and integrity, and of vision. If anthropology has been conceived, this single failure will surely not be enough to prevent its birth and development.

VIII

We must then turn, as *le Géographe* docks in Le Havre in June 1804, to ask what has happened in these four years in France. Have the ideas formulated by Degérando, and seconded by Jauffret and his society, taken root, and made the failure of Péron no more than a passing set-back to the new science?

Our first look uncovers promising signs of activity.[2] Daubenton gave a lecture at the *Ecole Normale* entitled 'Leçon sur l'Homme'. In 1800 to 1801, Lacépède gave a course of lectures in the general field of zoology, and in his opening address said: 'We are going to concern ourselves with man. . . . What more favourable

---
[1] Péron, 2.43, volume I, p. 10.
[2] See Hervé, 3.12.

moment to attain this end than that in which science is being especially directed towards the knowledge of man, in which naturalists, travellers, philosophers of the highest calibre, have just devoted themselves to the observation of man (they have just founded the *Société des Observateurs de l'Homme*), and in which the famous maxim of the wise men of Greece: *Know thyself*, has become the honourable motto of their illustrious association.' Later, Lacépède was to contribute the article *Homme* to the *Dictionnaire des Sciences Naturelles*, which was devoted mainly to physical anthropology. Jauffret himself, apart from his activities with the newly-founded society, gave a twice weekly course of lectures in the Louvre in winter 1800–1803, on 'L'Histoire naturelle de l'Homme'. At the same time, he was compiling some 'mémoires pour servir a l'histoire naturelle, morale et politique du genre humain',[1] no doubt wholly or partly for the purpose of his public lectures.

But we have to ask ourselves on what material all this work was based. And the answer is, of course, that it was based on the writings of past travellers, with all their faults. Something, indeed, may be achieved by this method, given sufficient industry. And Jauffret was industrious. His first four memoirs alone (covering only thirty-two pages) cite some sixty different writers. But, as has already been noticed, such industry will not replace fieldwork: and it was precisely with this in view that the *Société des Observateurs de l'Homme* had been founded.

Degérando's work was already published, and it made the point strongly enough. But a further publication was planned (though it never reached fruition) to which Jauffret composed an introduction read to the society in September 1802. In this essay, after recommending the study of physical anthropology, history, antiquity, and voyages, Jauffret turned to the topic which concerns us. As history enlightens social science,

[1] I.3.

he said, so anthropology enlightens early history. He spoke of the 'tribes which so little deserve the damaging scorn in which we hold them', and continued: 'There was a time when the desire to observe man counted for nothing in government-sponsored expeditions. The sole motive of scientific expeditions was to bring back from far lands animals, vegetables, and mineral substances. As for commercial expeditions, their only purpose was to go spreading our vices afar, and doing dishonour to humanity. The end of the eighteenth century opened a new path, and the beginning of a new century favoured the impulse which had been given. Following in the tracks of Cook, and of that no less illustrious traveller whom the society counts among its members (Bougainville), observers full of enthusiasm, correspondents of the society, have gone to study man in the vast theatre of the universe. Enlightened on the chief faults perpetrated by former travellers, and on the gaps in their accounts, they strove to do what their predecessors have not done.' Mention is made of Degérando's memoir. 'It was the task of the society to lay the first foundations of an enterprise whose importance cannot be mistaken, and whose success will be always on the increase; of an enterprise undertaken at the same time to do honour to the group of men engaged on it, and to the government that gives its sanction.'[1]

The theme is becoming hackneyed. For all the high words, the burden of research is here laid on Péron alone. And the same meeting at which Jauffret read his introduction was regaled with a curious assortment of topics of the kind which have already been noted. Bouchaud spoke on 'legislative errors which have been the chief source of the decadence of some powers'; Pfeffel on the origin of the word 'slave'; Legout on the customs and religion of the Hindus; Degérando on 'the Hermitage of Mount Vesuvius, or Meditation on solitude'; Sicard on the advantages to the science

[1] See Hervé, 3.11.

of man of observing deaf-mutes from birth.¹

This last is at least some sort of project of empirical research. And there was another at the same meeting: it was decided to award a prize for the best treatment of the following interesting topic: 'to determine, by general observations and by a selection of particular ones, what is the influence of different professions on the character of those who exercise them?' But, like Péron, the society seemed to prefer speculation to work. There is no sign that anyone entered for the prize.

One other extraordinary project was put forward by Jauffret in his opening address. Speaking of the interest of child psychology, he said that an attempt should be made to get government approval 'to make careful observations, for twelve to fifteen years, of four or six children, an equal number of each sex, kept from birth in the same enclosure, remote from any social institution, and left, for the development of ideas and of language, to natural instinct alone'. Jauffret's biographer cites the uncertain testimony of a female acquaintance of the pedagogue that this experiment was actually carried out, and that its results were collected by an unknown member of the society.²

The practical difficulties of such an experiment, apart from moral considerations, make it difficult to believe that it was in fact carried out. But it is interesting that it was proposed. We might trace a literary tradition back to Herodotos. More to the point, perhaps, is the impression of a boyish effusion of extraordinary, unconnected, and impracticable plans. There is none of the hard-headedness that research demands.

The internal weaknesses of the society are exaggerated by political pressures. Bonaparte is in a phase in which his face is set against colonial expansion. More, he has turned against the intellectuals. 'Idéologie', Destutt de Tracy's recently coined name for the new

[1] There is a report of the meeting in the *Magasin Encyclopédique* for 1802.
[2] See REBOUL, 3.21.

philosophy, has become a sign of political unreliability. In a few years, the soil in which it was natural to plant the *Société des Observateurs de l'Homme* has been fenced off. Climbing the fence was a good way of hampering one's career. And very few did climb it: none to water the frail growth of anthropology.

In June 1804, the *Société des Observateurs de l'Homme* uttered an expiring sycophancy: 'Whereas the foundation of this society dates back to the first months in which the reigns of government had been confided to the hands which assured France of prosperity without bounds;

'and whereas since that moment it has not ceased openly professing those principles whose bases it has found in the deepest study of the human heart and the social order, and which have at length prevailed for the well-being of the State;

'and whereas it is above all by offering to the public the first volume of its memoirs that it must give an unmistakable proof of its respectful devotion and of its high admiration for the august person of Napoleon;

'the society decrees that an approach will be made to his Imperial Majesty to request permission to dedicate to him the Memoirs of the Society, and to adopt the title *Société Impériale des Observateurs de l'Homme*.'[1]

This was the moral and actual end of the society, and incidentally the end of Jauffret's career in Paris. He had taken up and abandoned the administrative editorship of the *Dictionnaire des Sciences Naturelles*: he had been compelled to give creditors the manuscript of one of his public lectures as security for debt. No advancement offered. He retreated to Marseilles, as director of the museum of the town.

But, as has been noticed, his society had already been ailing for lack of the facts which it needed; and it failed to appreciate what a serious lack this was. We

[1] See Hervé, 3.11.

may profitably return to the satire published anonymously by Pierre-Edouard Lemontey in 1803.[1] It is a long and telling piece. At one point we find the report of the adjudicators of a prize awarded for a work on 'Apology for the Slavery of Women'. There were four hundred and sixty-eight bad replies, and the prize had been awarded to the worst, bearing the epigraph: 'The slavery of women is justified by reasons as good as those for the slavery of Negroes.' The author was present, and with pride claimed his reward. 'My name is Dominic Hangman, planter of Jamaica.' Throwing the golden chain which he had won to his poor, pale wife, he said: 'Take hold of that, Madam – I promised it to you; I was certain of my victory.'

It was an acute stroke of Lemontey to put the issue of slavery into his pillory of the *Société des Observateurs de l'Homme*. Members of the society had frequently referred to the rights of their fellow men, though a tone of patronage can be detected. And they should have done so for a particular reason; moral issues aside, the profession of anthropology as an enlightened and scientific interest in primitive peoples, does not consort with the support of slavery.

A conflict of attitudes was sometimes displayed in small matters. Péron, for example, later writing the official account of Baudin's expedition, said in complaint against the captain, that the expedition had rapidly run out of brandy, 'indispensable to the European sailor', and that they had been forced to resort to the evil liquor used only by the black slaves of Mauritius.[2] Péron seems to have disliked the associations of this drink, as much as its taste. Again, Jauffret was quite unconscious of the moral dubiety of his project to isolate and observe some children from birth.

But what of the issue of slavery? Adam Smith may

---

[1] 2.18.
[2] Péron, 2.43, volume I, p. 331.

have argued persuasively that free labour was in the end cheaper than slave labour:[1] but theories had no effect on the attitudes of French colonies. Slaves could not be dispensed with. Accordingly, the home government decided in 1802 to repeal the order made eight years earlier. The government speaker on this occasion defended the reintroduction of slavery as in the political interest of France, and in the interest of 'colonial agriculture, trade, of humanity, and enlightened philosophy'.[2] The government had a substantial majority.

And how did the *Société des Observateurs de l'Homme* stand on this issue? There was no stand; but we find one telling indication of the attitude of Degérando.

In 1802, a five volume work was published by V.-P. Mallouet on colonial administration.[3] In the following year, the *Magasin Encyclopédique* carried a favourable review of this work by Degérando.[4] Degérando cites with approval a passage recommending the neutrality of colonies in war – a passage which gives as one reason for this recommendation that if colonies take part in wars, the adversary may be forced to arm his slaves. And the result of this is that 'I become, against my own interest, the ally of our common enemy'. When we then read of Mallouet's basing the administration of colonies on the right of the citizen, and of his eloquence in defending 'the great interests of humanity and justice', we may be amazed that the author of the present work should lend himself to such mockery.

But the time-serving of Degérando, the sycophancy of Jauffret, and the superficial duplicity of Péron, effectively mark that withering of social anthropology of which we spoke earlier. But why did this failure occur? Did it just happen that Degérando, Jauffret, and

---

[1] 2.52, Book I, chapter VIII.
[2] See 3.15.
[3] 2.40.
[4] 2.35.

Péron lacked the application and integrity to nourish their progeny? Or was there a sickness of the times?

IX

What is the sickness of a time? It is a vague, and therefore dangerous notion, which may serve as no more than a vehicle for the writer's regret or judgment. I propose, however, to apply the idea in a determinate sense. I shall say that there is a sickness of a time, when, at that time, a set of ideas is prevalent such that any attempt to put them into practice leads to a conflict between one or more of those ideas and the rest. As an instance of such a case, consider the following passage from the first chapter of Mrs. Webb's autobiography:[1] 'My mother had been brought up in the strictest sect of utilitarian economists. In middle life, she had translated some of the essays of her friend Michel Chevalier, who represented the French variant of orthodox political economy, a variant which caricatured the dogmatic faith in a beneficent self-interest. And my mother practised what she preached. Tested by economy in money and time, she was an admirable expenditor of the family income: she never visited the servants' quarters and seldom spoke to any servant other than her own maid. . . . Her intellect told her that to pay more than the market rate, to exact fewer than the customary hours or insist on less than the usual strain – even if it could be proved that these conditions were injurious to the health and happiness of the persons concerned – was an act of self-indulgence, a defiance of nature's laws which would bring disaster on the individual and the community. . . . Only by the persistent pursuit by each individual of his own and his family's interest would the highest general level of civilization be attained. . . . No one of the present generation realizes with what sincerity and fervour these doctrines were held by the mid-Victorian

[1] 2.54.

middle class. "The man who sells his cow too cheap goes to hell" still epitomizes, according to John Butler Yeats, "the greater part of the religion of Belfast" – that last backwater of the sanctimonious commercialism of the nineteenth century. My mother's distinction was that she was free of the taint of hypocrisy; she realized the hopeless inconsistency of this theory of human nature and conduct.'

In this case, then, the 'faith in a beneficent self-interest' contains an inconsistency, since in recommending a certain economic system for the greatest individual welfare, it is also prescribing in practice actions which are against the welfare of other individuals.

Was there, then, at the time of Péron, Jauffret, and Degérando some sickness of this kind, such as to account for the withering away of anthropology? I believe that there was. The sickness lay in the ideal of *useful knowledge*. This liberal ideal is aptly conveyed in a passage of Rémusat's *Politique Libérale*:[1] 'The philosophy of the eighteenth century was simply the exaggerated expression of an individualism which shook off all traditional conventions, and all official maxims . . . . Taking root in certain minds that lacked discernment and moderation, and harnessed to the passions of an ardent or vulgar sensibility, fundamental errors could develop into systems that would justify violence and evil. There is some affinity between doctrines which calculate interests instead of weighing rights, which value the will more than the reason, which put justice on the side of the greatest number, and those disordered policies which have too often been believed to preserve the revolution while violating its principles, and which, pushing liberty to the point of licence, open the door again to tyranny. The task then is not merely to replace a Platonic love of truth at the summit of knowledge. To rid philosophy of the blight of a false method or of the excesses

[1] 2.48.

of polemic, is not merely to work for an ideal; it is to strengthen the starting point, illuminate the way, and ensure the progress of all those who carry general ideas into the affairs of the world, and who believe that in politics as elsewhere, science is above art, right above fact. Thus, since one can judge eighteenth century philosophy without betraying the French Revolution, one can, in correcting it by a better philosophy, continue to serve the revolution itself, and reconcile the useful and the true.'

The faith was that so long as the misguided pursuit of false knowledge had been abjured, as men ceased agitating themselves in metaphysical speculation, then the pursuit of knowledge and the pursuit of advantage were one and the same. To discover something true *is* to discover something of remote or immediate advantage to human society. Thus we find in this period societies for the promotion of 'useful knowledge', periodicals compiled by groups of 'gens utiles'.[1] Degérando is a founder in 1801 of the *Société d'encouragement pour l'industrie nationale*, and later of the *Société pour l'amélioration de l'éducation élémentaire*.

A detailed documentation of this faith is beyond the scope of the present introduction. But it was widespread and powerful, the more so since it was an assumption rather than an explicit article of belief. However, this creed too has an internal weakness: the pursuit of knowledge certainly may conflict with the pursuit of social advantage. When such a conflict arises, either one of the two is overridden, or it may be sophistically claimed that the conflict is apparent, not real; that if the discovery of nuclear weapons is an advancement in knowledge, then it must necessarily be a betterment of society; that if the Church deems the study of modern astronomy socially inexpedient, then it is necessarily not a genuine branch of knowledge.

Such conflicts did not fail to arise in their own way in

[1] e.g. 2.1.

early nineteenth century France. They were bound to, until that ideal of useful knowledge was abandoned, and the sickness thus cured.

A good case to illustrate the point, however briefly, is that of education. Since Rousseau's *Emile*, theoretical discussion of principles of education had been widespread. But according to the ideal of useful knowledge, theory must be united with practice. And so it was, for example, in the case of Pestalozzi – and in France, in their own way, of Jauffret, of Degérando, of Cuvier.

The customary high words are to be found. A reviewer of G.-M. Raymond's *Métaphysique des Etudes* wrote: 'The author concludes with some considerations on moral teaching: he could not finish better than by staying on wisdom, that health of the soul, that only true knowledge which was the sole object of study of the earliest philosophers, the goal of all their efforts, as the fair name of philosophy should remind all those among us who are concerned with the study of nature and of man.' But knowledge is practice. The reviewer concluded: 'Such are the chief points made in this work, which deserves to be read and thought over by all those concerned with the instruction of the young.'[1]

In the same spirit, the philosopher Maine de Biran wrote to Degérando: 'It is you, my dear Degérando, who taught me never to separate the moral end from our speculative researches on human faculties.'[2]

And Maine de Biran was an educational pioneer,[3] inaugurating in 1807 a school in Bergerac (where he was sub-prefect), the primary section of which was directed by a pupil of Pestalozzi. It seems an excellent case of 'philosophy in action', to borrow a telling phrase from a work of Degérando on the education of deaf-mutes,[4] – of the exercise of the ideal of useful knowledge.

[1] 2.37.
[2] 2.39.
[3] See 3.17.
[4] 2.14, vol. II, part III, chapter IX, p. 534.

Yet there were those to question the social utility of such educational advance. Bonaparte's indifference to Pestalozzi's visit in 1802 (he said: 'I have better things to do than discuss the ABC.') soon turned to distrust: would the 'overeducation' of the poor lead to social unrest? In terms of the ideal of useful knowledge itself, this was not merely a politically relevant question, but also an intellectually vital one.

Le Publiciste published an article in 1808 rebuking the French for their comparative lack of interest in the great advances made by Pestalozzi. But these 'advances' had to be disqualified if they should have social disadvantages. Maine de Biran himself could write, in a subsequent letter to *le Publiciste* drawing attention to his own work in this field, 'I should not wish to give these simple people superfluous enlightenment, which would make them discontent with their station, but a fit education which would teach them to live in the condition in which fate has placed them, better, wiser and happier.'

The mere occurrence of the expression 'superfluous enlightenment' is striking. It shows at once the hold of the ideal of useful knowledge, and its capacity to generate conflicts. In this case, the conflict is felt even by the pioneer; it must have contributed to the comparatively quick failure of the project.

Degérando himself had been associated with it. As secretary-general to the Minister of the Interior, and friend of the philosopher, he was asked by Maine de Biran for patronage, advice, and help. It is not insignificant that Degérando seems to have done nothing more than suggest that the sub-prefect write directly to Pestalozzi.

Here then is an instance of the conflict of which we have already spoken. Intellectual schemes, even when being put into effect, may be hindered or thwarted by the application of criteria of utility demanded by the ideal of useful knowledge. In other terms, 'philosophy in action' must sometimes be put out of action. And the ideal is such that this curtailment may itself be represented as in some way *intellectually* necessary. We saw how a government speaker recommended the reintroduction of slavery by appealing to the interests of 'enlightened philosophy'. And the words are not mere hypocrisy. They are a clear symptom of the sickness which is now being exposed.

X

Is it then a sickness which struck the new anthropology? It can, I think, be readily shown that it did. For the most forceful and impressive programme of the new science was that given by Degérando in the present text. The exordium of this text is devoted to a rapturous evocation of vast commercial and political advantages accruing to France from Baudin's expedition, and in part from the practice of anthropology. It should now be clear that these words are not window-dressing. They provide a central impetus to the very conception of the new science.

Thus when the impetus ceases, when colonial projects are no longer entertained, the science fades away, being no longer 'useful'. The more so since Baudin's expedition, which had carried the heavy burden of symbolizing political and scientific aspirations, was widely regarded as a scandalous failure. In fact, of course, its achievements were very considerable, although the government's programme was not quite completed. It came to be held a failure partly because of a growing disenchantment with the projects which it had been sent to carry out. From being a symbol of hopes, *le Géographe* became a scapegoat. The more so since Bory de St. Vincent, and later Péron and Freycinet, who wrote the official account of the expedition, engaged in spirited libel of their dead captain. No one had survived to speak up for Baudin, and the myth of his inadequacy was perpetuated. It was in the interests of the former commissioners of the

Institut also to ensure that in spite of their responsibility for the planning of the expedition, no blame devolved on them. Cuvier was quite ready, in a report to the *Institut* in 1806, to praise the completeness and perfection of Péron's anthropological observations, and to hint at the culpability of Baudin.

But, it must be repeated, the expedition was not a scandalous failure, and the question of culpability does not arise. That it was felt to arise may be traced in part, as I have suggested, to the loss of interest in colonial enterprise, and the consequent loss of weight of the project of an empirical anthropology. The link between these two changes deserves further emphasis. It is to be noticed that no one at this time thought of going off on his own to do field-work, though this would not have been especially difficult. The science was conceived as a government enterprise, and as an associate of the government's political and commercial ambitions.

However, Péron lived until 1810, and for all that had been said, the science still kept a weak life in him. We read of a grandiose project: fifteen years of travel in Northern Europe, Asia, India and America were to provide the material for an *Histoire philosophique des divers peuples considérés sous les rapports physiques et moraux*.[1]

It is unfortunate that Péron never lived to set foot outside France again. The tradition might have been continued. Yet we could not have expected much of the levity of his projects, and of his fickleness in carrying them out. Indeed, this levity was typical of the ideal of useful knowledge. Degérando too was known to his contemporaries as a verbose man who poked his nose into everything; so was he described to Maine de Biran before the meeting of the two men.[2] Ste-Beuve described him as 'one of those writers who spin out like macaroni, getting longer without ever breaking'.

[1] 2.43, vol. II, p. 449.
[2] 2.39.

The ideal was fertile in intellectual projects, which were weeded out by utility as a hoe. As we have now seen, five years after its planting, anthropology, already ill-tended by an indifferent set of gardeners, was classified as a weed, uprooted, and thrown on the heap.

The European in face of the aboriginal turned back once more to prejudice, though the prejudice might be favourable. An article in the *Magasin Encyclopédique* in 1813 declared: 'It is to be believed that the whites will be persuaded to conceive and to treat as men, beings who differ from them only by their colour.'[1]

The differences that do exist were no longer to be a matter of research. Degérando's text was forgotten for three generations. He lacked the vision to break through the ideas of his time, yet he had the merit to recommend a method of field-work in anthropology uncorrupted by the prejudices in which he himself shared. His text on the observation of savage peoples deserves the attention of those interested both in the history, and in the practice of anthropology.

[1] 2.38.

Considerations on the Various Methods to Follow in the Observation of SAVAGE PEOPLES

Advertisement

These considerations are addressed to Captain BAUDIN, correspondent of the society, about to leave for his expedition of discovery, and to the various observers accompanying him; they are addressed also to Citizen LEVAILLANT, who is going to attempt a third expedition in the interior of Africa. Since it is possible that both have occasion to encounter peoples at very different degrees of civilization or barbarity, it seems the right course to provide for any hypothesis, and to make these CONSIDERATIONS so general that they can be applied to any society differing in its moral and political forms from those of Europe. The leading purpose has been to provide a complete framework comprising any point of view from which these societies can be envisaged by the philosopher. It has not been supposed that certain simple questions that can easily be foreseen should be omitted, when they were necessary to the completeness of the whole.

IT seems astonishing that, in an age of egoism, it is so difficult to persuade man that of all studies, the most important is that of himself. This is because egoism, like all passions, is blind. The attention of the egoist is directed to the immediate needs of which his senses give notice, and cannot be raised to those reflective needs that reason discloses to us; his aim is satisfaction, not perfection. He considers only his individual self; his species is nothing to him. Perhaps he fears that in penetrating the mysteries of his being he will ensure his own abasement, blush at his discoveries, and meet his conscience.

<small>Importance of the study of Man in general.</small>

True philosophy, always at one with moral science, tells a different tale. The source of useful illumination, we are told, like that of lasting content, is in ourselves. Our insight depends above all on the state of our faculties; but how can we bring our faculties to perfection if we do not know their nature and their laws? The elements of happiness are the moral sentiments; but how can we develop these sentiments without considering the principle of our affections, and the means of directing them? We become better by studying ourselves; the man who thoroughly knows himself is the wise man. Such reflection on the nature of his being brings a man to a better awareness of all the bonds that unite us to our fellows, to the re-discovery at the inner root of his existence of that identity of common life actuating us all, to feeling the full force of that fine maxim of the ancients: 'I am a man, and nothing human is alien to me.'

But what are the means of the proper study of man? Here the history of philosophy, and the common voice of learned men give reply. The time for systems is past. Weary of its centuries of vain agitation in vain theories, the pursuit of learning has settled at last on the way of observation. It has recognized nature as its true master. All its art is applied in listening carefully to that voice, and sometimes in asking it questions. The Science of Man too is a natural science, a science of observation, the most noble of all. What science does not aspire to be a natural science? Even art, which men sometimes contrast with nature, aims only to imitate her.

The method of observation has a sure procedure; it gathers facts to compare them, and compares them to know them better. The natural sciences are in a way no more than a series of comparisons. As each particular phenomenon is ordinarily the result of the combined action of several causes, it would be only a deep mystery for us if we considered it on its own: but if it is compared with analogous phenomena, they throw light each on the other. The particular action of each cause we see as distinct and independent, and general laws are the result. Good observation requires analysis; now, one carries out analysis in philosophy by comparisons, as in chemistry by the play of chemical affinities.

Man, as he appears to us in the individuals around us, is modified at the same time by a multitude of varying circumstances, by education, climate, political institutions, customs, established opinions, by the effects of imitation, by the influence of the factitious needs that he has created. Among so many diverse causes that unite to produce that great and interesting effect, we can never disentangle the precise action that belongs to each, without finding terms of comparison to isolate man from the particular circumstances in which he is presented to us, and to lift from him those adventitious forms under which, as it were, art has hidden from our eyes the work of nature.

Now, of all the terms of comparison that we can choose, there is none more fascinating, more fruitful in useful trains of thought than that offered by savage peoples. Here we can remove first the variations pertaining to the climate, the organism, the habits of physical life, and we shall notice that among nations much less developed by the effect of moral institutions, these natural variations are bound to emerge much more prominently: being less distinguished by secon-

Of the observation of savages in particular.

dary circumstances, they must chiefly be so by the first and fundamental circumstances belonging to the very principle of existence. Here we shall be able to find the material needed to construct an exact scale of the various degrees of civilization, and to assign to each its characteristic properties; we shall come to know what needs, what ideas, what habits are produced in each era of human society. Here, since the development of passions and of intellectual faculties is much more limited, it will be much easier for us to penetrate their nature, and determine their fundamental laws. Here, since different generations have exercised only the slightest influence on each other, we shall in a way be taken back to the first periods of our own history; we shall be able to set up secure experiments on the origin and generation of ideas, on the formation and development of language, and on the relations between these two processes. The philosophical traveller, sailing to the ends of the earth, is in fact travelling in time; he is exploring the past; every step he makes is the passage of an age. Those unknown islands that he reaches are for him the cradle of human society. Those peoples whom our ignorant vanity scorns are displayed to him as ancient and majestic monuments of the origin of ages: monuments infinitely more worthy of our admiration and respect than those famous pyramids vaunted by the banks of the Nile. They witness only the frivolous ambition and the passing power of some individuals whose names have scarcely come down to us; but the others recreate for us the state of our own ancestors, and the earliest history of the world.

And even should we not see in savage peoples a useful object of instruction for ourselves, would there not be enough high feelings of philanthropy to make us give a high importance to the contact that we can make with them? What more moving plan than that of re-establishing in such a way the august ties of universal society, of finding once more those former kinsmen separated by long exile from the rest of the common family, of offering a hand to them to raise them to a happier state! You who, led by a generous devotion on those far shores, will soon come near their lonely huts, go before them as the representatives of all humanity! Give them in that name the vow of brotherly alliance! Wipe from their minds the memory of cruel adventurers who sought to stay with them only to rob or bring them into slavery; go to them only to offer benefits. Bring them our arts, and not our corruption, the standard of our morality, and not the example of our vices, our sciences, and not our scepticism, the advantages of civilization, and not its abuses; conceal from them that in these countries too, though more enlightened, men destroy each other in combat, and degrade each other by their passions. Sitting near them, amid their lonely forests and on their unknown shores, speak to them only of peace, of unity, of useful work; tell them that, in those empires unknown to them, that you have left to visit them, there are men who pray for their happiness, who greet them as brothers, and who join with all their hearts in the generous intentions which lead you among them.

In expressing here everything that we expect of your careful and laborious work, we are far from wishing to underestimate the many services done to society by the explorers who have gone before you. Had they merely prepared the way, by their brave undertakings, for those who were to follow them, and provided valuable guidance, by that alone they would have earned a great title to our gratitude. But they began to establish some communication with savage societies; they have reported to us various information on the customs and language of these peoples. It is merely that, divided by other concerns, and with a great impetus to discover new countries than to study them, constantly moving when they should have stayed at rest, biased perhaps by those unjust prejudices that cast a slur in our eyes on savage societies, or at

Faults in the observations made up to the present.

least, witness of our European indifference for them, they did not sufficiently devote themselves to bringing back exact and complete observations; they have met the invariable end of those who observe in a precipitate and superficial manner – their observations have been poor, and the imperfection of their reports has been the penalty of our carelessness.[1] Since man's curiosity is aroused more by the novelties that strike his senses than by any instruction that his reason may gather, it was thought far more worth while to bring back from these countries plants, animals and mineral substances, than observations on the phenomena of thought. So naturalists daily enriched their specimen cases with many genera, while philosophers spent time in vain disputes in their schools about the nature of man, instead of uniting to study him in the arena of the universe.

Let us review the main faults of the observations on savage man made by these explorers, and the gaps that they have left in their accounts. When we realize what they have not done, we shall see better what remains to be done.

The first fault that we notice in the observations of explorers on savages is their incompleteness; it was only to be expected, given the shortness of their stay, the division of their attention, and the absence of any regular tabulation of their findings. Sometimes, confining themselves to the study of some isolated individuals, they have given us no information on their social condition, and have thus deprived us of the means of estimating the influence which these social relations might have on individual faculties. Sometimes, pausing on the smallest details of the physical life of the savages, they have given us scarcely any

First fault.

---

[1] It is unnecessary to give warning that the critical reflections that we are making on the accounts of explorers are levelled at the usual run of these accounts, and consequently admit notable exceptions. Far be it from us to wish a lessening of the admiration due to men like Cook, Bougainville and others. In this respect, you will have preceded us: it has been your first concern to study their writings.

details of their moral customs. Sometimes, describing the customs of grown men, they have failed to find out about the kind of education received in childhood and youth: and above all, preoccupied almost entirely with the external and overt characteristics of a people, of its ceremonies and of its dress, they have generally taken too little care to be initiated in the far more important circumstances of its theoretical life, of its needs, its ideas, its passions, its knowledge, its laws. They have described forms rather than given instructive reports; they have marked certain effects, and explained scarcely any causes.

Further, such insufficient observations have not always been very certain or authentic, whether because they have sometimes been too particular, and explorers have wished to judge a society by a few of its members, a character by a few actions, or because they have sometimes confined themselves to hearsay, to the stories of the Savages whom they met, and who perhaps were not properly understood, perhaps not well-versed in what was asked, and perhaps had no interest in telling the truth, or at least in making it known in its entirety. _{Second fault.}

We should add that these observations have been badly ordered, and even in many cases quite without order. The explorers had not enough understood that there is a natural connection between the various facts that one gathers about the condition and character of societies, that this order is necessary to the precision of the individual facts, and that often some of them should serve as preparation for the others. We should study effects before trying to go back to first principles; observe individuals before trying to judge the society; become acquainted with domestic relations inside families before examining the political relations of society; and above all we should aim at full mutual understanding when we speak to men before basing certain conclusions on the accounts that we claim to have received. _{Third fault.}

Often explorers have based the accounts that they bring us on incorrect or at least on dubious hypotheses. For example, they habitually judge the customs of Savages by analogies drawn from our own customs, when in fact they are so little related to each other. Thus, given certain actions, they suppose certain opinions or needs because among us such actions ordinarily result from these needs or opinions. They make the Savage reason as we do, when the Savage does not himself explain to them his reasoning. So they often pronounce excessively severe judgments on a society accused of cruelty, theft, licentiousness, and atheism. It were wiser to gather a large number of facts, before trying to explain them, and to allow hypothesis only after exhausting the light of experience. *Fourth fault.*

In the case of the accounts of explorers there is another cause of uncertainty, a fault of language rather than of imperfect observation, namely that the terms used to pass on to us the results of their observations are often in our own language of vague and ill-determined meaning. Consequently, we are in danger of taking their accounts in a way which they did not intend. This happens particularly when they try to record the religious, moral, and political beliefs of a people. It happens too when instead of giving a detailed and circumstantial account of what they have actually seen, they limit themselves to summary descriptions of the impressions which they received, and of the general judgments which they inferred on the character of peoples. Yet this drawback could easily have been avoided by making it a policy either to describe things without judging them, or to choose expressions whose sense is more agreed, or to give a precise stipulation of the sense in which one intends their use. *Fifth fault.*

This is not the place to enumerate the inaccuracies springing from a lack of impartiality in explorers, from prejudices imposed by their particular opinions, from the interests of vanity or the impulse of resentment. *Sixth fault.*

The character of the worthy men today devoting themselves to this noble undertaking is a sufficient guarantee that such a stamp will never shape their accounts. But explorers with the purest and most honest intentions have often been led into error about the character of peoples by the behaviour they meet with. They have inferred too lightly from the circumstances of their reception, conclusions about the absolute and ordinary character of the men among whom they have penetrated. They have failed to consider sufficiently that their presence was bound to be a natural source of fear, defiance, and reserve; that reasons of policy might exaggerate this unusual circumspection; that the memory of former attacks might have left dark prejudices in the mind of such peoples; that a community might be gentle and sociable, and yet believe itself in a state of natural war with strangers whose intentions are unknown; and finally that for a just estimate of the character of a tribe, one should first leave time for the reactions of astonishment, terror, and anxiety bound to arise in the beginning to be dispelled, and secondly one should be able to be initiated into the ordinary relations which the members of the community have with each other.

But of all the regrets left by the accounts of the explorers who went before you, the strongest is their failure to tell us of the language of the peoples visited. In the first place, the scanty information which they do give lacks precision and exactness, whether because they fail to record how they went about questioning the Savages, or because they themselves have often taken little care to pose the questions properly. The demonstrative and natural gestures which they have used to ask the Savages the names of objects were often themselves liable to considerable uncertainty; one cannot know if those who were questioned understood the gestures in the same way as the explorers who were using them, and so whether they were giving proper replies to their questions. Further, to provide us with Seventh fault.

some useful and positive ideas of the idioms of savage peoples, it was wrong for explorers to limit themselves as they did to taking at random names of various objects with scarcely any relation between them; at least a family of analogous ideas should have been followed up, when it was impossible to make a record of the whole language, so that some judgment could be made on the generation of terms, and on the relations between them; it was not enough to be content with some detached words; but it would have been sensible to record whole sentences to give some idea of the construction of discourse. Further, one should have discovered whether these words were simple, or composite, as their length would often lead us to suppose; whether they were qualified by any articles or particles; and finally whether they were inflected or remained in the absolute, and whether they were liable to any kind of grammatical laws.

Failing to acquaint themselves thoroughly with the idiom of savage peoples, explorers have been powerless to draw on perhaps the most interesting ideas that could have been available. They have been unable to pass on the traditions that such peoples may preserve of their origin, of the changes that they have undergone, and of the various details of their history; traditions which perhaps would have thrown great light on the important question of how the world was peopled, and on the various causes of the present state of these societies. They have been unable to explain the significance of a mass of ceremonies and customs which are probably no more than allegorical; they have given us bizarre descriptions which tickle the idle curiosity of the many, but which offer no useful instruction to the philosophically minded. Lacking the means to carry on connected conversation with such peoples, they have been able to form only very hazardous and vague ideas of their opinions and notions; finally, they have been unable to provide us with these data, as revealing as they are abundant, that the language of a society

Eighth fault.

presents on its way of seeing and feeling, and on the most intimate and essential features of its character.

The main object, therefore, that should today occupy the attention and zeal of a truly philosophical traveller would be the careful gathering of all means that might assist him to penetrate the thought of the peoples among whom he would be situated, and to account for the order of their actions and relationships. This is not only because such study is in itself the most important of all, it is also because it must stand as a necessary preliminary and introduction to all the others. It is a delusion to suppose that one can properly observe a people whom one cannot understand and with whom one cannot converse. The first means to the proper knowledge of the Savages, is to become after a fashion like one of them; and it is by learning their language that we shall become their fellow citizens.

Observations to make. 1. Signs of the Savages.

But if there is a marked lack of good methods even for learning well the languages of neighbouring civilized nations; if this study often requires much time and effort, what position shall we be in for learning the idioms of savage tribes, when there is no dictionary, no spokesman to translate to us, and no shared habits and common associations of ideas as in the case of the former languages, through which explanations can be made? Let us not hesitate to say that the art of properly studying these languages, if it could be reduced to rules, would be one of the master-works of philosophy; it can be the result only of long meditation on the origin of ideas. We shall confine ourselves here to making some general remarks; the reflective thought of the enlightened men to whom we address them will assure their development, and direct their application.

The most important thing to observe in the study of the signs of Savages, is the order of the enquiry.

Since the articulate language of savage peoples, according to the information which we have about it, is composed of signs almost as arbitrary and conventional as our own, it is clear that to establish an initial intercourse with them, we need to go back to signs which are closest to nature; with them, as with children, we must begin with the language of action. *[sidenote: Language of action. Various types of gesture.]*

In the language of action or gesture, three kinds of sign must be distinguished; demonstrative signs, whose only function is to fix the attention on an object that is present; descriptive signs with which, when the object is not present, we imitate its shape, its size, its movements; and finally, metaphorical signs, which help us, when we cannot imitate and depict an object, to reproduce at least the circumstances connected with it in our memory, recalling, for example, the effect by its cause, or the whole by one of its parts.

Of these three kinds of sign, the *demonstrative* is that whose effect is most sure, and least subject to ambiguity, when it can be used. It is with such signs, therefore, that we should begin; it is to them that we must have recourse in cases of doubt. We must think of *describing* only when we cannot *point out*.

The usefulness of *descriptive* signs will depend on how effective the descriptions are. Now the effectiveness of a description depends on the skill with which three conditions have been observed: the imitation first of the most striking and obvious qualities of objects, secondly of those most peculiar to them, qualities which are thus more suitable to distinguish the objects with which they could be confounded; and finally of those which must have been particularly noticeable to the individuals with whom one is speaking, whether by the nature of their dispositions or by the effect of the circumstances in which they were placed.

Metaphorical signs are most of all liable to uncertainty, and most difficult to interpret in a precise way.

Yet one is often compelled to have recourse to them. Accordingly, if the explorer uses them, he will overlook nothing that could make them more expressive; he will avoid supposing too readily that the Savage entertains associations of ideas analogous to his own. If it is the Savage who is using them, the explorer will be careful to encompass faithfully all the accompanying circumstances, and to adduce previously known habits of the people, which may assist explanation.

We cannot recommend too strongly to the explorers for whom these reflections have been prepared, that they should become particularly acquainted with the methodical signs used so successfully by citizen Sicard to establish his first communication with deaf-mutes. For the deaf-mute is also a Savage, and Nature is the only interpreter to translate for him the first lessons of his masters. However, it is important to notice that one must not expect that the gestures used in the case of deaf-mutes should always have a comparable effect in the case of savage peoples; in fact, the meaning of these signs depends above all on the habits of those to whom one is speaking; these habits in turn are largely the effect of the circumstances in which they are situated. Now the circumstances of the deaf-mute brought up among us are not shared by the Savage who has never left his forests. The explorer will therefore make a point of choosing such of these gestures as relate least in their expression to accidental circumstances. They will be able to modify them according to the habits which they must suppose the savage tribes to have; their aim will be to grasp the general method of the signs used by the Teacher of deaf-mutes, rather than to repeat scrupulously all the gestures that he actually uses.

Of the gestures of Deaf-mutes.

It would be desirable if one could accumulate all the natural and imitative signs found among the Savages and bring back to us drawings of them with exact explanations of the interpretation given to each.

When the explorer has obtained in this way, by the use of the language of action, a preliminary means of communication with the Savages, he will proceed to the study of their articulate language. *Articulate language.*

Here, the order to be followed is that closest to the generation of ideas. *Order in which it should be learnt.*

The first words that they will aim to know will be the words for the objects that are both the simplest and the most palpable, like the various parts of the body, and the material substances that the savage can see. *Elements of language. Primitive ideas.*

Their first aim, then, must be to ask only the names of *things* or substances, and not of qualities, actions, or relations, since it is these that offer least ambiguity and which are least changed in discourse. *Nouns.*

They will then pass on to the names of sensible qualities, like colours, smells, tastes, hardness, and softness. *Adjectives.*

From there they will move to the names of sensible actions, like *walk, drink, eat, fish*, and so on, the ideas of which are always more complex, avoiding any association with circumstances of time, place, or relation, in order to have the verbs in their absolute form. *Verbs.*

They will conclude with the terms used to express relations, and which have given rise in our language to prepositions and adverbs. Since the idea of a relation always arises from the comparison of two or more objects, they will take care to put these objects under the eyes of the Savages, and to arrange them in such a way that the relation for which they are asking the word is that which most naturally strikes their attention. *Prepositions.*

After fixing these first elements, they will be able to ask the terms given to more complex ideas, like those of a village, a forest, an army, of war, and so on, taking care to specify exactly the essential circumstances on which these complex ideas are based. *Complex ideas.*

No doubt the Savages cannot have a large number of abstract ideas, since they have not had the oppor- *Abstract ideas.*

tunity to carry out systematic comparisons. But the need to simplify leads men so naturally to abstraction, even unknowingly, and to forming ideas of genus and species, that the Savages cannot be completely without them. To question them in this field, we must begin with the easiest abstractions, that is, those which require less repetition of comparisons. Thus, in showing them two trees of different species, we shall soon discover if they have a distinct name for each species, and one for trees in general; and likewise for animals. By pointing out to them at the same time the movement of an animate being, and that of a stone, we shall find out whether they have a name for the abstract idea of movement. As they meet these questions, we shall proceed to more remote abstractions, by making them carry out more extensive comparisons.

The ideas with which the Savages would be least occupied are those belonging to reflection and in the province of moral psychology and logic, like *thought, judgment, will, sorrow* and so on. To these ideas we shall come last, applying greater care and precision; it is here above all, when asking them about such ideas, that we must be on our guard against the habits belonging to our particular education, and that we must avoid imputing to the Savages the arguments of our philosophers. We must try to penetrate what they think, and not claim to make them think as we do. The moral ideas which should be the first subject of our questioning will be those closest to sensible ideas, like *desire, hope, fear, joy, death* and so on. These enquiries will be made by describing the external actions that accompany these modes of existence, and always ensuring that they do not give the name of the *action* instead of that of the hidden *impression* determining it. Reflective ideas.

Having in this way more or less fixed the nomenclature of elementary terms, we shall be well-advised to have whole speeches delivered, and to note very carefully: Connected speech.

1. the order in which words are placed;

2. the changes which these words may have undergone in their association with each other;

3. the auxiliary expressions which will have been used to make connections, and to perform the exact function for which each one will have been applied.

So it will be possible to answer the following questions: *Questions to resolve.*

Does the idiom of such and such a savage people comprise composite words, or has it only radicals?

Are composite words formed according to the law of analogy?

Are the radicals simple and monosyllabic?

Are they strongly onomatopoeic?

Are nouns regularly declined according to *gender*, *number*, and *case*?

Are the names of qualities or *adjectives* varied with the noun which they qualify? Have they *comparatives*, *intensives*, *diminutives*, etc.?

Are the names of actions, or *verbs*, conjugated according to *person*, *tense* and *mood*, or do they simply remain in the absolute?

Are there *articles* and *conjunctions*, and of what kind?

Has this people any idea of the laws of syntax?

Has it any feeling for the niceties of harmony and oratorical beauty?

It would be useless to follow the order which we have just adumbrated without taking certain indispensable practical precautions against ambiguity. *Precautions to take.*

It is above all in the manner of questioning the Savages that great care must be applied; for such questions ordinarily have vague points which make them liable to several different interpretations.

So, for example, if one points out an object, the Savage may believe that he is being asked the name of that object, or simply that of one of its properties, or that of the use for which it is intended, or of its position, or merely of its kind.

Now, it is by repeating these questions in different ways, in different circumstances, to different individuals, that one will come to remove the uncertainty of the replies.

When the Savages reply with words as long as those reported by Cook, or even with words of several syllables, it would be to the point to find out whether the Savages give any special sense to each syllable, by repeating each separately, and whether, in consequence, what one took for a single word was a composite expression.

After collecting whole speeches, we shall do well to change their order sometimes, and alter them in several ways, by adding or removing some word, to find out whether their effects are always the same, or how these effects are modified.

Since the idioms of the Savages are probably very scanty, it is inevitable that each term should have for them more than one meaning. You will take care to gather these various meanings, in order to judge, by the extension which they give to the senses of the words, of the association of their ideas, and of their use of analogy.

One part of the idiom of the Savages which it would be especially important to complete as soon as possible is that concerning numbers. It will not be enough to know the highest quantities to which they give names; it will be necessary to discover also the whole sequence of their words for the natural number series, and the methods which they use to designate higher quantities than those to which they have given distinct names, provided that they in fact have some method for this. *Numeration.*

It will be right to observe whether they modify the words given to the ideas of quantity to yield ordinals, like *first, second, tenth, hundredth,* and to form concrete terms, like *dozen, score,* etc.

There are few savage peoples which have not tried to capture in more or less crude figures the image of objects which they wished to remember. It would be interesting to observe the dominant features of these figures, so that one could know too in the case of these *Painting and Writing.*

objects what circumstances have most forcibly struck the attention of the savages. When one visits peoples already in the early stages of civilization, one will find a richer field for such research; careful observation will determine whether they have begun to use these paintings as a means of communication; whether they have made from them some kind of hieroglyphic system; what the idea of the hieroglyphs might be, and what their main laws are; and finally, whether they have any idea of a script, that is, of conventional figures representing either ideas or language; or at least whether they have any inkling of its usefulness to us.

It seems, at least, that all peoples have resorted to certain emblems, sometimes based on explicit conventions, sometimes on more or less close analogies, to replace long speeches. Such are the signs of fires or of war, of rupture or alliance; allegories are associated with them, like various sorts of trophy, civil or religious practices and ceremonies, and particularly dances, those dances sometimes so mysterious for a stranger, and perhaps so apt to instruct us in the history and character of peoples; finally, these peoples are sure to have various signals to warn each other over long distances, during a hunt, a journey, or a battle. The explorer will no longer confine himself to the simple description of all these conventions; he will try as far as possible to reach an understanding of the sense attached to them, the effects they produce, and the origin from which they spring. Emblems, allegories, and signals.

Although this long and difficult study of the signs used by the Savages is, no doubt, not necessary in its entirety for the observation of their political and moral state, and although it is not necessary to await the completion of this task before beginning the observation of other objects, yet the progress that the explorer makes in this first respect will give him more rapid and certain means of instruction in the second. 2. State of the Savages and first, of the individual. His physical existence.

It is not our present task to make a detailed study of the procedures to be followed in gathering every type of information about the state of savage peoples. The right intentions and the experience of explorers will be more helpful to them in this matter than our vague indications. We shall therefore confine ourselves to giving them a tabulated summary of the most important points at which their observations should be directed, to presenting them with the order which seems to us most appropriate, and to reminding them that the results reported to us will be valuable and useful in proportion to their degree of completeness.

All these observations can be grouped in two main categories: the state of the individual, and that of the society.

The first objects to notice in the case of the individual are the circumstances of his physical existence.

The first case is the kind of climate in which he lives. You will not be satisfied with observing the degrees of heat and cold; you will try to discover the properties of the atmosphere which he breathes, to determine its elasticity, its purity, its condensation, its humidity, and so on. <small>Climate.</small>

The next case is the quality and quantity of his ordinary food and drink. A careful analysis of the water with which he quenches his thirst, and a test of his distaste for our own food, will be to the point. <small>Food.</small>

We shall be given more positive information about the physical strength of the individual savage.[1] You will discover what burdens he is capable of lifting, carrying, or dragging; what are his most successful muscular movements; how quickly he can run; how far he can travel without rest; how good he is at swimming; what physical exercises he ordinarily undertakes; you will observe how he climbs trees, crosses ditches, climbs rocks, and so on. <small>Physical strength and action.</small>

You will report how many hours he sleeps; whether <small>Sleep.</small>

[1] When we say: the *individual savage*, the *savage*, the *savage people*, it will be understood that it is not our intention to speak of the savage in *general*, nor to suggest that savage peoples are all of a single common type: this would be absurd. It is simply a short way of mentioning the *individual savage* or the *savage people* under the observation of explorers at the time.

his sleep is deep, whether it is peaceful or seems disturbed by dreams; what the character of these dreams might be; whether he has a fixed hour for sleep; whether it disturbs or displeases him to go without sleep; what position he takes up when he rests or goes to sleep.

How strongly the Savage feels hunger, thirst, and fatigue; what effects these needs bring about; whether he has a leaning for idleness or takes pleasure in activity. Needs.

The philosophical traveller will make a careful study of the dreadful practice of cannibalism, and perhaps will give us some way, if not of justifying, at least of excusing the errors of the human species. They will tell whether cannibal peoples eat only their enemies beaten in war; whether they add to this action any other cruel practices, and whether they entertain ideas of vengeance in the custom; whether they seem to be very afraid of the same fate; whether there are any regular accompanying ceremonies; whether they find it at all repugnant to eat the flesh of their friends or of strangers; or whether they think by their act to inflict any suffering or shame on the soul of the massacred man. Cannibalism.

The clothes of Savages are generally very well described by explorers; this is nearly always their main observation, often the only one; but one should not confine oneself to observing their costume; you should investigate how repugnant they would find it to change their customs or adopt ours; and whether they have any reason for wearing what they do, any circumstance which has made them adopt their present style; for habit and imitation only establish what is already there, and there certainly must have been a first origin of these customs. Thus the need to protect oneself from insects, or from the effects of heat and cold, must contribute considerably to the custom of some savage peoples of anointing their bodies. Finally, you should find out whether clothes vary with Clothes.

age or status, whether they give evidence of authority or wealth, and whether there is any idea of adornment, and if so how important it is.

We shall ask the explorers to tell us of the moral effects which may accompany the illnesses of the Savages; to tell us whether they resemble those with which we are familiar, and in what they differ; to tell us whether the Savages endure suffering with calm, courage, and patience; whether the source of their endurance is in apathy of character, in an ignorance of the future which admits no fear of the duration of pain, or in some reflective concept like a kind of glory and vanity in the peaceful endurance of suffering, as among the Savages of America. We shall ask at what point their moral faculties are changed by these physical disturbances; whether they become thereby more accessible to fear or credulity; whether they fear death, and what may be the principle of their fear or confidence in this respect.

Moral effects of illness.

Is it true that the phenomenon of madness is never found among Savages, or is it just that examples are very rare? If an example is found, it is a matter of importance to collect all the circumstances of cause and effect, in order to compare them with our observations in the case of civilized man. It may be presumed, at least, that you are bound to come across examples of imbecility, a state which depends much less than the former on the passions of the soul, and on moral impressions, and which is nearly always to be attributed to a natural organic defect. So you will take care to determine the degree of imbecility, and the external characteristics accompanying it. You will look for the first occasion which will seem to have determined it; you will distinguish its various kinds, if there are several. You will observe in particular whether this imbecility takes the form of senility, at what age it is present, how common it is, at what point it is noticed, etc.

Imbecility and madness.

The physical education given by the Savages to their

Physical education.

children is one of the points of which explorers have left us in deeper ignorance. It may be simply that these peoples take no care about the development of their children, and leave them entirely to nature. But then we should at least have been told what effects this has, whether the children are more or less subject to disease, whether they learn to marshal their strength more readily, whether mortality is greater or less among them, what dominant instincts one notices in these children, etc. But if on the other hand, as seems probable, their parents take some care of them during the first years of their life, we hope to be told some details of the matter; what precautions the mother takes for her new-born child; at what age the child is weaned; what type of food the child is given at first; in what posture it is put to sleep; at what point the mother begins to leave it to itself; what routine she has for washing the child; whether she tries to protect it from heat and cold; whether she helps it in illness; finally, how the children are first exercised, their occupations in domestic life, the tasks they are given, the enthusiasm shown in performing them, and their success in the venture.

The length of life of the Savages will provide a field for several questions. Do they live to more or less the same age, or is there some appreciable difference between the lengths of their lives, and how marked is that difference? What approximately is their average life-span? How far do the examples of the greatest longevity go? What are the most frequent causes of death among them? *Longevity.*

All these observations bearing on the external circumstances of life are quite easy to gather, if the explorers have leisure to spend some time among the Savages, and can cultivate familiarity with them. But if, after their attempt to investigate man as a physical being, they turn their attention to the observation of his intellectual and moral nature, it is at this point that they will encounter a host of difficulties, that they *The individual considered as an intellectual and moral being.*

will need to beware of inferences that are too precipitate, of observations that are too superficial, of the prejudices that spring from our habits; it is at this point that they will need above all to formulate their judgments with the strictest circumspection, their accounts with the greatest clarity and the most rigorous precision.

The first object of their attention will be the senses of the Savage. They will make a detailed investigation of the various sensations, and concentrate especially on answering the following four questions: 1. Which of their senses are the most exercised, the most active, and the most discriminating? 2. What circumstances may have led to the more marked development of one particular sense? 3. What is the degree of development of each of their senses compared to what is usual among us? 4. To what class and species of sensation do they attach most pleasure?

<small>Sensations.</small>

The development of one particular sense should be judged by a number of factors: 1. the art with which two or more sensations are distinguished; 2. the tenuity of sensations that can be noticed; 3. the number of sensations that can be simultaneously grasped; 4. the speed with which the operations are carried out; 5. the capacity to prolong them for a more or less long period without fatigue; 6. finally, the precision of the judgments which sometimes accompany them. This is what makes up, for example, what we call the exactness of a visual observation, and the art of judging distance.

Observation will be directed with most care to the condition of the senses of touch and sight, as the most important. It is to be observed whether the natural state of the organs, as well as practice, contributes to the frequent perfection that one finds in the senses of savage man; they will find out whether blindness and deafness are more or less common than among us; and they will not fail to determine the moral effects of these two conditions, that is, the degree of gloom, helplessness or idleness which may accompany them, and the means adopted to compensate for the lack of an organ.

Our ideas are nothing more than elaborated sensations. Thus after having in some way recorded the materials on which the Savage works, the observer will try to discover the transformation to which they are subjected. Now sensations are transformed in two ways, by combination, and by abstraction. By following this double path, one will discover the exact scope of the set of ideas of the individual savage, and its limits; we shall be told of the point to which the art of generalizing has been carried; of the excursions they have made in the realm of moral ideas; there will be answers to the following important questions: *[Ideas. Their nature.]*

Has the Savage the idea of a principle of feeling and motion situated in himself?

How does he conceive it?

Has he the idea of anything simple and indivisible, and consequently immaterial?

Has he formed the abstractions of being and not-being, finite and infinite, duration and eternity, possible and necessary?

Has he any idea of the *beautiful*, and is it conceived other than as what *pleases* him?

Has he any idea of the *good*, and is it conceived other than as what is *useful* to him?

Does he imagine what he has never seen?

Has he the idea of lands other than his own, of a universe other than that in which he lives? etc. etc.

No doubt, the observers will not believe themselves to have solved these great problems if they have restricted themselves to questioning the Savage, and receiving in reply a vague sign or term. There will be a plain need to submit the savage intellect to some more stringent test. They will not suppose the Savage to have reached a certain degree of abstraction without having seen him carry out the comparisons required; they will suppose him to have a certain combination *[Their generation.]*

only when he is able to give an account of it. When the observer finds in the Savage some general or reflective idea, he will do his utmost to find in what circumstances it was formed; he will try in a way to wrest from the Savage the secret of his intellectual history, and to bring back for us a record of the generation of his ideas.

The great law of the association of ideas is one of the chief bases on which rests the intellectual system of man. Thus, after discovering the nature of the ideas with which the Savage is provided, the observer will make a study of how they are associated. Here, he will have three things to note; first, how easily these associations are formed, secondly, how persistent they are, and how easily evoked, and third, their scope. Since needs are so many centres to which associations of ideas relate, it is above all by paying attention to needs that the observer will discover the point to which associations of ideas can extend.

<small>Their association.</small>

How does the Savage make a judgment about objects which are not, at the time of the judgment, within reach of his senses? Is it simply by habit, that is, from the inclination to believe that things must always repeat themselves in the same manner as hitherto? Does he use analogical inductions, and what range does he allow this type of judgment? Can one discern in him any sort of instinct like that seen in animals, namely a disposition to do what is useful to him, or to avoid what is harmful, even when no experience could have taught him of the effects which must follow? What influence does imitation exercise over his judgments and his actions?

<small>Opinions and judgments.</small>

What impression is made on the Savage by the spectacle of the ordinary phenomena of nature? Does he go back from the knowledge of effects to the supposition of certain causes, and how does he imagine these causes? Does he allow a first cause? Does he attribute to it intelligence, power, wisdom, and goodness? Does he believe it to be immaterial?

<small>God.</small>

Does he suppose it to have a fixed abode? Does he furnish it with physical agents? Does he consider it as a providence, that is, as a being that watches over him and over nature? Does he believe it eternal? Does he suppose it capable of understanding him, penetrating his thoughts, being swayed by his prayer? Does he allow several of these causes? Does he endow them with equal power? Does he suppose them to be at one with each other? By what attributes does he distinguish them? Does he put between the first cause and himself invisible secondary agents? What ideas does he form of them? Does he attribute a principle of action and of feeling to the stars, to plants, to the elements, and so on? What is his idea of animals?

What impression is made on the Savage by the spectacle of the extraordinary phenomena of nature? How does he explain them? Does he imagine himself to have had any sort of existence before his appearance on earth? Does he have the idea of any purpose for which he believes himself set in the world? How does he conceive death? Does he think of a change in existence and abode? Does he believe in an immaterial existence? Does he put any limit on this existence, and allow a time when he shall return to nothingness? Is this idea distasteful to him? Does he attach to the future life any idea of punishment or reward? On what does he found these ideas? Does he regard himself as free, that is, as capable of choosing at his will among various actions that present themselves to him? Or does he in fact allow some idea of fate?

Ideas on his existence.

Immortality.

The faculties are to the understanding as strength is to the body. Both develop in exercise, and are judged by their effects. Thus, the degree of vivacity and energy of a man's *imagination* will be judged by the readiness with which he makes resolutions, by his accessibility to fear or hope, by his cleverness in finding new means to achieve his aims, and finally by his leaning to describe or depict what he thinks of or experiences. The imagination is the first faculty to be

Faculties. Imagination.

studied in the Savage, since it is the one which nourishes all the others. The imagination is always the first faculty to develop in the individual; thus the development of this faculty will be the easiest indication for ascertaining the level occupied by that individual in the scale of intellectual advancement. Next comes *attention*. We shall learn how well the Savage can concentrate; what motives control this faculty in him; what objects it leads him more especially to remark; it is by following the thread of his needs that these observations can be established with suitable precision. *Memory* is grafted on attention; for one remembers only things to which one has paid enough attention. Thus the studies to be made of these two faculties in the Savage will be closely linked. We shall learn if he easily retains what he has seen, heard or experienced; if their trace lasts long; how far back his memories go; in what order they are retained; what gaps they leave between them; to what pivots the series that they form are attached, and so on. *Foresight* in turn must spring from memory; for it is simply the faculty of making application of our past experience. Note will therefore be taken of how the Savage can use the experience that he acquires, how far into the future he can look, how far he turns to account his current circumstances, how he is able to take precautions against events, how he learns to correct his own errors when he comes across some mistake in his conduct. Finally, of all the faculties, that which develops most easily, which seems most properly to belong to the civilized man, is *reflection*, that is, the faculty by which we turn back on ourselves to give ourselves an account of our feelings, our thoughts, and to penetrate into the innermost secrets of our manner of being. It would be interesting to know whether the Savage does not possess at least some beginning of so noble a power, or whether he remains always a stranger to himself; it would be necessary to observe whether, when his activity is not

Attention.

Memory.

Foresight.

Reflection

drawn out by the objects surrounding him and connected with his needs, he then reverts to a kind of vegetative torpor, or whether he enjoys some existence of his own. For the rest, the most certain proof that can be attained about the level of reflective activity enjoyed by the Savage will be in the character of his language.

With the formation of complex and abstract ideas, with the play of the intellectual faculties, there develops in man a second order of needs that we call *reflective*, because they are not immediately connected with his existence. The observer will seek to give a precise definition of the nature and extent of these needs in the Savage. We shall learn the extent of his propensity to be curious, the effects on him of surprise, his liability to fear or the torments of anxiety; we shall learn how he is attracted by amusement or pleasure, whether he seeks strong emotions and varied sensations; we shall learn of his self-control, of the fearlessness or weakness that he shows in face of danger, of the confidence or arrogance stirred in him by success, of the pride or shame that his introspection produces, of his regrets for unsuccessful actions, of the pleasure he takes in the awareness of his own forces, of any idea that he may have of his inferiority, and of a stage of development happier than what he has attained, and so on.

Reflective needs.

It is no doubt unnecessary to warn observers that they must not restrict themselves to establishing these enquiries in the case of a single individual, but that it is necessary to repeat them in a large number of cases, and to compare the results gained. Explorers generally speak only of a simple common type for each country; and they suppose that an entire people belongs to it. Is there then no variety between the various members of a savage society? And is not this variety, though much less apparent, no doubt, than that seen in civilized societies, nevertheless real and interesting? Will not a careful investigation of these beings so far from us, lead one to notice in their faculties, habits,

Variety.

ideas, opinions, and inclinations differences produced by age, sex, organism, and circumstances? There too, would not a young man be more impetuous and active, a woman more timid and reserved, and an old man more prudent? Would not temperament give rise to livelier passions, or softer dispositions? Cannot bodily structure alone give one man a marked superiority over another? Is the quality of life absolutely uniform? Must not each man find in his own experience either the occasion of some learning or the source of some need that is peculiar to himself?

After having observed the individual as he is in himself, one will follow him in his relations with his fellows; and here there will be a new order of research.

The Savage in Society.

We have had in Europe several examples of individuals found in the middle of forests, and who appear to have had virtually no communication with other men. But such examples cannot stand for the savage state. It is the last degree of humanity. In probability, there is not any type of Savage among whom one does not find at least some beginning of society. But explorers will have to find out whether there are not to be found among them some individuals condemned by chance to an entirely solitary life; and in this case they will carefully note all the particular characteristics evinced by these men.

The first society to which man is called by the voice of nature, and by the impulse of reciprocal needs, is domestic society, namely, that which is composed of the family.

Domestic society.

Explorers will observe whether this first union has the marks of a regular society, and whether there is any subordination between its members. Does the father have any authority? What are the effects, the period and the extent of this authority? On what principle does it appear to be based, and what idea of it has he who exercises it, and those who obey him? What respect have young people for the old, and how is it

Authority of fathers.

evinced? What degree of gratitude is kept by children for the authors of their days?

What is the force and character of the bond between brothers? Is there any precedence of age among them? To what point do the relations of kinship extend and keep any influence? In what way are they observed? Do the members of a single family unite for work, for hunting, for food? Then what law and order is observed among them? Is each individual free to retire as he wishes, or by what bonds is he retained? Kinship and fraternity.

The domestic condition of women can be considered from several points of view. The first to present itself is that of their dependence, or of the consideration shown for them. In this respect, Savages have sometimes presented quite different spectacles. In general, however, it seems that consideration for the female sex is an effect of civilization. The observations of explorers will teach us how far this idea has any foundation; they will teach us what right a woman has on common property, what work she has to do, what protection she is given; finally, they will teach us whether even in the most savage countries, the female sex preserves something of that sweet and secret power, rooted at once on her weakness, on her sensitivity and on her charms. Women. Their condition.

The second point in considering the women concerns their conduct with respect to the laws of modesty. Two things must be noted here; their knowledge of these laws, and their care in observing them. Are there, in fact, any savage tribes so brutish that the women have absolutely no sense of modesty, that they completely lack inhibitions, and that they go before men without a blush? Or is it in fact that they have some ideas of duty in this respect, but are simply very ready to fall short of them, because of temperament, opportunity, example, or persuasion? Modesty.

This leads to some questions on love and marriage.

The story of love among savage peoples would present a picture as strange as it is interesting. Its Love.

origin, character, signs, effects, sacrifices, vengeance – how much all these must differ from what is the case among us. But is the parallel to their advantage or ours? Is the emotion of love in Savages purely physical? Does it allow any idea of confidence, privilege, devotion, of moral association? Does it cease with its enjoyment, or how lasting is it? Is it fastened on a single individual, or indiscriminately on several, and does it then carry with it no idea of infidelity and inconstancy? Are the favours of women considered solely as the recompense of love, and what value do men give it? What reciprocal considerations accompany the feelings? Is it the man who usually makes advances? Does he often have difficulty?

The ideas of marriage, that is, of a legitimate union between man and woman, are established only in a society already to some extent developed. But the point at which such an establishment begins is very important to note. It is equally important to determine all its circumstances.

Is marriage considered only as the result of the free consent of the spouses? Is the will of the parents enough to compel the union of the children? Or are both factors combined? Is marriage considered as a civil act in which society has an interest, and if so what part does society take in it? Is marriage considered as a religious act, and if so in what respect do religious ideas contribute to it? Marriage.

What reciprocal duties are set up between the spouses, and what sanctions are there? Does paternity contribute much to their ties? How are they modified by age? Is it a general custom among savage peoples to stop all communication with the female sex during the period of its ordinary discomforts? Its character. Its effects.

Is there any example among the Savages of the indissolubility of marriage, and on what principle then does it appear to be founded? Among those who divorce, one should know the number and frequency of divorces, the motives giving rise to them, the forms Divorce, polygamy.

accompanying them, and the effects which they produce. Note will be taken of the force and character of jealousy in husbands and wives; whether adultery is punished in the one case or the other, and what the punishment is. In noting whether polygamy is the custom, one will examine to what point it extends, what the origin and reason for it appears to be, what its effects are, with respect to customs, population, the education of children, domestic harmony, and so on.

It is certain that one cannot expect to find among the Savages any very interesting particularities on the moral education of children. However, there are several circumstances worthy of note. What is the degree of attachment and the nature of the interest that the parents feel towards their children? To what point do they feel their guardianship and severity to go? Is it the father or the mother who takes most care of them? To what age does this care last? Is it equal for all the children, or do they show any preference? How do children learn their language? How are they initiated into the moral ideas which their parents may have? Finally, how quickly are the passions and the intellect developed in them? Moral education of children.

From domestic society, let us pass on to society at large, that which is formed by the aggregation of families; it is presented to us under four different kinds of relations – political, civil, religious, and economic. Let us begin by political relations, which are the basis of all the others. Society at large.

First, what are the internal bonds of society, and the foundations on which rests the union of its members? Is there any gradation in the formation of this society, that is, is it sub-divided, as among us, into several partial aggregations, more closely linked together, like clans, boroughs, or castes, and what are the relations and limits of these particular associations? Is there any distinction of rank? What is its basis? Is it connected with birth? By what prerogatives is it shown? How many different degrees has it? What is the number of Political relations. 1. Internal.

magistracies and of magistrates? Are their functions hereditary or elective, and what would the circumstances of this election be? What is the nature and extent of their authority? What is their hierarchy? In what spirit is this hierarchy observed? What limits check them? Do they hold their posts for life or for a term? Are they liable to be deposed, and if so how does this take place? Is supreme authority in the hands of one man or of several? In the first case, is it absolute, arbitrary? What circumstances accompany it? How is it transmitted? On what objects is it deployed? In the second case, how are the chiefs chosen? How do they reach agreement among themselves? Are their operations collective, or does each in fact have a separate administrative sphere? Magistrates. Their entitlement. Their authority.

What ideas have these peoples of authority and its rights? How do they look on their chiefs? What affection, confidence, or submission is shown to them? What homage is done them? With what pomp are they surrounded?

What are the effects of these institutions? To what point does the union of members of society extend? What solidity does it have? What are the occasions, the circumstances, and the effects of civil discord? Are revolutions frequent, and bloody? Have the laws need of a general sanction? Are there even any laws, or does the will of those in power take their place? How are the laws preserved? Its effects.

What attitude does a tribe have to those surrounding it, and living under another authority? Are they naturally at war, or do they live ordinarily in peace? 2. External.

If they are naturally at war, what is the source of this mutual disposition? Is it antipathy? Is it a result of vengeance and memories? Is it rivalry? Is it the desire of conquests? War.

If wars are not typical, what ordinarily gives rise to them? Causes.

Who has the right to declare war? Is this declaration preceded by any negotiation, or at least any formality? Circumstances.

What are these formalities, or what is the character of these negotiations?

Are wars universal, that is, does the whole people take part? Are they bloody, and long? Do they suspend all other forms of contact between the peoples? Do they suspend the awareness of natural rights?

Have these peoples any kind of military art? What is their discipline in war and battle? Do they march in some order? Do they act in concert during battle? Do they use surprise tactics or open attacks? Are the battles long, and is victory disputed for a long period? What precautions do they take? What resources do they deploy when surprised, or after defeat? Military art.

We cannot make the complaint that ordinary explorers have left us in ignorance either of the kind of arms used by the Savages, or of the use which they make of them, but what is the nature and degree of courage shown by these peoples? Is it impetuous or steadfast? Are they raging or fearless? What ideas do they have of courage itself? What feeling do they have of honour, glory, and independence? Arms.

Courage.

To what point do the results of war extend? Are the women, the children, and the homes prey of the conqueror, and what is their lot at his hand? Does the conqueror take prisoners? What treatment does he impose on them? What is the state and condition of slaves? What feelings do they have? Is there any other slavery but that of conquest? Effects of war.

How does war end? Is it by complete destruction, or expulsion of the vanquished? Or by some kind of peace-making? How is peace proposed, adopted, guaranteed, and what are its ordinary conditions? Peace.

Are there any alliances between neighbouring tribes? What gives rise to them, and what purpose do they have? What provisions most usually compose them? What is their term? What is the basis of their strength? What idea have the peoples of their duty to abide by their undertakings, and what is their reciprocal good faith? What talents do they develop in these Alliance.

negotiations? What means do they put to the best use for their success?

What welcome does a savage people give to strangers quite unknown to it, like Europeans? What is the reason for this reception? Here careful precautions must be taken before making a judgment. One must try first to ascertain that the reception given one by a savage people is not the effect of memories left by other strangers; and then it would be necessary to know also what the actual conduct of these strangers towards the people was. Even when no memory could influence the reception that one receives, are there several ways of explaining the same reception? Fear and ferocity equally can put arms in the hand of the people visited; good nature, trust, timidity or perfidy can equally lead him to accord strangers a favourable welcome. Finally, ferocity, defiance, or the sweet virtue of hospitality, are themselves moral phenomena whose causes we should, as far as possible, seek to penetrate. *Strangers. Hospitality.*

Civil institutions have as their object to guarantee for members of society their possessions, and their life, most precious of all possessions. *Civil relations.*

Has a savage people the idea of property? If it is a grazing or hunting tribe, it lacks no doubt the idea of territorial property; but then, has it not at least the idea of property in its instruments, and in the objects won by its efforts? *Property.*

Is the punishment of wrong among a savage people left to the vengeance of the aggrieved party? If this is so, in what cases is this vengeance arrogated? What vengeance is taken Does the culpable man recognize it as right? Or does the quarrel appear to be no more than the strife of force against force? If the punishment of wrong is confined to some authority, what is this authority? What crimes does it recognize? How does it ascertain them? To what punishment does it submit them, and by what principle does it appear to determine its sentences? *Crimes.*

The first object of note, in considering the group in its economic relations, is the fertility of the territory inhabited by a people, and the greater or less abundance of resources provided by its land. *Economic relations. Territory.*

Then it must be noticed how this territory is used, and its resources exploited; whether any cultivation is practised or known, whether at least fruit is picked from trees, whether there are any domestic animals, whether their flesh or their milk is used for food, or nourishment is sought only in hunting or fishing. *Primary industry.*

It is quite difficult to explain how a hunting people is marked off by a distinction so pronounced and durable from an agricultural people. How is it that the idea does not come to such a people to try the food offered by the fruits of the earth, and then to attempt to reproduce them? What hidden obstacle holds it back in the sphere of so laborious and painful an existence, making the satisfaction of its first needs depend on a long and perilous chase? Such is the problem that we submit to the wisdom of the explorer. It is at least to the point to try to make them adopt a happier and more convenient way of life, by giving them some examples of it, if one should not succeed in teaching them the art of cultivation, to make them feel its benefits. If one cannot succeed, then it would be proper to try to penetrate the motive of such a singular repugnance.

Cook and other explorers have tried to transplant our domestic animals among various savage tribes. It is important to find out what they have done with them; and in the places where these strains have been destroyed or dispersed, one should find out for what reason they have been abandoned in this way. We emphasize these considerations, because if one found some means to transform savage peoples to the condition of *herdsmen* or *husbandmen*, one would, no doubt, open before them the surest route that could lead them to the advantages of civilization. *Attempts.*

The type of life led by a people is necessarily connected with its manner of habitation. Thus we shall have to learn whether its homes are fixed or variable; whether it often changes its dwelling place; what motives control its travels. *Nomadism. Abode.*

The second type of industry whose development should be studied is that whose object is needs of the second order, needs of convenience, like the construction of huts, and the making of clothes. The aim will be to describe the methods followed by the Savages and the procedures which they use; but one will attempt to see whether they try to perfect their skill in these undertakings, or why they do not do so; some efforts will be made to make them set about it better, and the means of doing so will be indicated. *Industry of the second order.*

The third type of industry consists in the preparation of tools. Here, the two most important things for the Savage are metals and fire. If they know metals, it should be found out how they fit them for their use. If they do not, one must observe how they substitute for them; one must see if they would like to learn to use them. As for fire, ignorance of it attests without doubt a state furthest removed from civilization, and it is unnecessary to recommend explorers to obtain this benefit for them. But even those tribes which use fire do not know all its effects; and this it would be quite interesting to examine. *Auxiliary industry.*

The construction of the skiffs and canoes used by the Savages, of their hunting and fishing implements, the description of the tricks and procedures that they use, of their way of navigating, and so on, are objects generally quite well described by travellers, since vulgar curiosity is more roused by them. Yet if possible you will not overlook the task of completing these descriptions and sketches, and above all of bringing back to Europe some patterns of the various instruments of the Savages. It would be interesting to know whether and how a savage People marks the passing of years, months, days, and hours.

Does a savage People never have any idea of commerce in its relations with neighbours? How readily does it engage in barter with strangers it visits? On what principle is this barter based? What price and value have objects for the tribe? Is it a matter simply of what is needed? Is any value given to surplus goods? Are there any attempts to draw advantage from the demand for a commodity? Does the savage readily dispose of things for which he has some use? Does he show good faith in these transactions; or if he is in bad faith, does he have any awareness of his wrong-doing? Most travellers have treated trade with savage Peoples as a gamble, or a mere means of establishing themselves in their midst in order to dominate. A philosophical traveller would be much more far-seeing. He would see in this trade a means of leading the people to civilization. In fact, our help is almost indispensable in this process; and only need can bring them close to us. So initial barter will make early communications easier; these contacts will perhaps serve to inspire in the Savage some new desires which will bring him still closer to us. Always well received, well treated, witness of our happiness, of our riches, and at the same time of our superiority, he will perhaps attach himself to us from gratitude or interest, will join in some alliance with us, will call us among his people to teach them how to reach our own condition. What joy! What a conquest, if some hope were open to us of exercising a gentle and useful influence on these abandoned Peoples, and to recreate in the Southern Seas the astonishing revolution of Paraguay!

<small>Commerce.</small>

It is quite striking to see sometimes people with scarcely a subsistence concerning themselves with their pleasures, and giving great importance to them. No doubt this kind of observation will excite the curiosity of travellers. They will study also the pleasures of the Savages, because this is a part of their life. They will examine their songs and their musical instruments; will try to find out if they have any idea of poetry; will

<small>Arts of amusement.</small>

ascertain whether their ears can appreciate perfect harmony; they will describe for us its detail those luxuries which are sometimes so extraordinary, and endeavour to penetrate the ideas attached to them.

The last and perhaps the most important of the topics provided for the observer by economic relations will be population. It will be necessary to ascertain first its density, and then its rate of growth, or decrease, and finally the real causes of such increase, or decadence. Population.

We have already spoken above of the notions that a people may have of religion and morality; here it remains only to consider the external social effects which these ideas produce. Moral and religious relations.

You will observe whether the Savage knows pity for weakness and sorrow, and if he requites good turns; you will observe the extent of these feelings in him, and if he is capable in addition of that generosity which repays a good turn by sacrifice. Does he also respond to the good turn with gratitude? How long does this gratitude last, and what are its outer signs? To what point does he consider himself obliged to his benefactor, and what sort of horror of ingratitude does he show? Generous virtues.

One will observe whether he is capable of putting up with offence, and the limits of this patience; the nature of his vengeance; whether he can be swayed from it; whether it exceeds the offence; whether there is any idea of justice attached to it, as to a sort of talion; whether he sometimes rises to the point of feeling the merit of forgiveness, and whether he is capable of gaining any hold over the passions of his heart. Strong virtues.

The traveller will note how far the hearts of the Savages may be susceptible to the affections which unite men; whether they give themselves up to that noble sentiment of friendship of which such peoples have often given us touching examples. Then he will study the character of such friendship, its origin, its effects, its signs, its length. Happy if he brings back for Affections.

Friendship.

philosophers some new proofs of the existence of that sublime instinct which draws man to his fellow, and of its inner inherence in our nature!

The feeling of friendship should perhaps be considered as the origin of all social affections; for goodwill pauses on what is at hand before going further; it is directed to the individual, before embracing society. What is patriotism in the heart of the Savage? Is it a feeling of affection for all those who live with him in a common society? Is it attachment to the soil on which he lives, to the life that he leads, to the habits by which he is ruled? Is it a return to his own interest? What is the force of this patriotism, and by what outer signs is it displayed? Would he sacrifice himself for the good of his society? What need does he have of liberty, what shame does he attach to slavery, and what hate does he have for arbitrary and despotic power? Is he also familiar with the ambition for power, and what form does it take for him? Patriotism.

Does the Savage regard the outer cult and ceremonies of his religion as necessarily connected to the idea which he has of a supreme Being or of his duties towards that Being? Is it with the intention of doing honour, of obtaining mercy, of giving thanks, that he ordains a cult to the supreme Being, or does he believe that he will thereby add to the enjoyments of that Being, by assimilating it in some way to himself? Religious ceremonies.

How many priests are there? In what way are they chosen? What consideration, what privileges, what authority are they given? Are they supposed to have any power over nature, any faculty of penetrating the future, or discovering the unknown? Have these priests any special education? Do they appear to be in good faith? Are they in general more moral than the rest of the community? How do they live in its midst? Do they practise medicine, and according to what ideas? Does their influence seem salutary? Do they show themselves disposed to support any projects of improvement or progress? Or are they rather interes- Priests.

ted in maintaining their people in ignorance and barbarity?

It will not be enough to have described, as one ordinarily does, the form of the temples, and the shape of the idols which are the objects of a people's veneration; we must be informed of the ideas which that people attaches to those idols, and those temples, provided that it does so. You will ascertain if we have here the ultimate object of his worship, or if he considers these objects simply as signs. *Temples. Idols.*

It will be the same with the various ceremonies, which, however odd they seem, or rather precisely because they are very odd, must have had some special reason.

Has a savage people fixed feast days? What is the occasion, what merits these feasts? The birth of children, marriage, death, burial, election of magistrates, war, peace, general calamities – are those the occasions of religious activities? Of what kind? Are there any which are repeated daily? Do they say common prayers, and what are they? Do they have any formula of malediction for their enemies? *Religious behaviour.*

What form of worship of the dead is found among a people, and what respect does it have for its tombs? *Tombs.*

The final, and no doubt the most difficult object of the traveller's curiosity will be to penetrate the traditions of savage peoples. They will be questioned on their origin, on the migrations which they have undergone, on the invasions to which they have been subjected, on the visits which they have received, on the important events that have taken place among them, on the progress which they have been able to make in respect of industry or political force, on the institution of the customs current among them. It may be that only very vague stories can be extracted from them; but a small number of facts can throw precious light on the mysterious history of these nations. *Traditions.*

We shall not finish without recommending to the travellers to bring back for us if they can Savages of both sexes, some adolescent and some infant, and to prepare them, by the best treatment, for the adoption in store for them.

Above all, it would be desirable if a whole family could be persuaded to come back with them. In that case, the individuals composing it, less restricted in their habits and saddened by their losses, would better preserve their natural character. They would agree more easily to settle among us; and the relations between them would make the spectacle of their life at once more interesting and more instructive for us. We should have in miniature the model of that society in which they were reared. So the naturalist is not content to bring back a branch, a flower that is soon withered; he tries to transplant the whole tree or plant, to give it a second life on our soil.

We are aware that the totality of problems here posed for the explorer's wisdom calls for a huge amount of work, whether because of the number and the very importance of the questions, or the detailed and painstaking observations that each one demands. We are aware that this work is surrounded by all kinds of difficulties, and that one must expect to meet great obstacles in the first relations that one wishes to establish with the Savages. For these peoples cannot penetrate the real intentions of those who approach them, they cannot easily distinguish their friends from their enemies, and those who bring help, from those who come to invade their territory. But we may rightly expect anything of the patience, the perseverance, and the heroic courage of the travellers to whom today we bid farewell; we are assured of it by their personal character, by the intentions animating them, by the dazzling proofs which they have already vouchsafed. Oh! What have they not already done for science, what noble course have they not already run! It was worthy of them still to defer its term, and to go on to complete so fine a work! Estimable men, as we salute you here on the eve of a departure soon to come, as we

<small>Conclusion.</small>

see you tear yourselves from your land, your family, and your friends, and leap beyond the limits of the civilized world; as we dwell on the thought of the fatigues, the privations and the dangers which await you, and of that long exile to which you have voluntarily condemned yourselves, our souls cannot resist a deep emotion, and the movement of sensibility in us is joined to the respect which we owe to so noble an undertaking. But our thought is settled in advance on the term of that undertaking; and dwelling on this prospect, all our feelings are mixed in that of admiration and enthusiasm. Illustrious messengers of philosophy, peaceful heroes, the conquests which you are going to add to the domain of science have more brilliance and value in our eyes than victories bought by the blood of men! All generous hearts, all friends of humanity join in your sublime mission; there is in this place more than one heart which envies you, which groans in secret that inflexible duties keep him on these shores, who would put his glory in following your path and your example. Our prayers at least will follow you across the Ocean, or in the lap of the desert; our thoughts will often be with you, when below the equator, or near the pole, you gather in silence precious treasures for enlightenment. We shall say to each other: 'On this day, at this hour, they are landing perhaps on an unknown land, they are perhaps penetrating to the heart of a new people, perhaps they are resting in the shade of antique forests from their long sufferings; perhaps they are beginning to enter into relations with a barbarous people, to eliminate its unsociable suspicions, to inspire in it a curiosity to know our ways and a desire to imitate them, and perhaps they are laying the foundations of a new Europe.' Oh! who will tell in fact all the possible or probable results which may spring one day from these fine undertakings? I speak here not only of our fuller specimen cases, our more accurate and extensive maps, of our increased knowledge of the physical and moral history of the world, of the name of France taken to unknown shores! Think of the other bewitching prospects still offered to the reeling imagination! Trade extended by new relations; the navy brought to perfection by greater experience; journeys made easier by discoveries; our political grandeur increased by new colonies or new alliances! Who can tell? Perhaps whole nations civilized, receiving from civilization the power to multiply themselves, and associate themselves with us by the ties of a vast confederation; perhaps broader and more useful careers open to human ambition, talent and industry; these peoples of Europe, daily contesting at the cost of their blood some narrow strip of land, expanding at pleasure in more beautiful terrain; perhaps a new world forming itself at the extremities of the earth; the whole globe covered with happier and wiser inhabitants, more equally provided for, more closely joined, society raising itself to more rapid progress by greater competition and reaching perhaps by these unexpected changes that perfection on which our prayers call, but to which our enlightenment, our methods, and our books, contribute so little! . . . Vain chimerae perhaps; but chimerae to which our long unhappiness, our sad dissensions, and the sight of our corruption, yet give so much charm!

. . . At least it is certain that these brave enterprises, directed to the most obscure parts of the Universe, lay up for posterity a new future, and that it is only for the wisdom of our descendants to gather the abundant fruits of this course that you are going to open. See how much the discoveries of Columbus changed the face of society, and what amazing destinies bore that fragile vessel to which he trusted himself! It is true, this grand revolution has not all been to our advantage, still less to that of the peoples to whom it has given us access. But Columbus put in the New World only greedy conquerors; and you are proceeding towards the peoples of the South only as pacifiers and friends. The cruel adventurers of Spain brought only destruction before them, and you will spread only good deeds. They served but the passions of a few men, and you aspire only to the good of all, to the glory of being of use! This glory, the sweetest, the truest, or rather the only true glory, awaits you, encompasses you already; you will know all its brilliance on that day of triumph and joy on which, returning to your country, welcomed amid our delight, you will arrive in our walls, loaded with the most precious spoils, and bearers of happy tidings of our brothers scattered in the uttermost confines of the Universe.

SOURCES

Primary Unpublished Sources

ARCHIVES DE LA MARINE, PARIS

1.1 *MS. sér.mod. BB⁴ Campagnes 995*
Plan of the commission of the Institut de France for Baudin's voyage, dated 4 floréal an VIII.

1.2 *ibid.*
'Expériences nautiques et observations diététiques proposées pour l'utilité de la navigation et de la santé des marins', by Bernadin de St. Pierre.
[A résumé of this work appears in the *Mémoires de l'Institut de France, classe des sciences morales et politiques*, tome IV, pp. 58–61.]

BIBLIOTHÈQUE DE L'ACADÉMIE DE MÉDICINE, PARIS

1.3 *MS. 165*
A bound volume of papers of Jauffret put in order by Robert-Marie Reboul. Their interest merits a detailed note. The first item is a group of 'mémoires pour servir à l'histoire naturelle, morale et politique du genre humain'; the second comprises two lectures from Jauffret's 'Cours d'histoire naturelle de l'homme'. In the analysis below, Reboul's page numbers are given, followed, in the case of the first item, by the two sets of numbers given by Jauffret to the memoirs, and his titles.

1	XXI	(1)	Histoire de l'écriture hiéroglyphique avec des considérations sur l'idée d'une langue universelle.
15	IV	(2)	Preuves que les peuples méridionaux ont un penchant beaucoup plus fort pour les boissons et les substances échauffantes et enyvrantes que ceux du Nord.
25	V	(3)	Sur le goût de plusieurs peuples pour les viandes et les boissons grasses.
27	VI	(4)	Sur le penchant de plusieurs peuples pour l'ivresse.
33	VII	(5)	Sur quelques embellissements des dents, usités chez plusieurs peuples.
36	VIII	(6)	Sur l'irritabilité sympathique des peuples faibles, et sur plusieurs phénomènes qu'il faut expliquer par elle.

45	IX	(7)	Sur le goût de plusieurs peuples qui mangent des poissons pourris et de la viande salée, surtout dans la zone torride, et sur l'aversion de plusieurs peuples pour le sel.
49	X	(8)	Sur le penchant de plusieurs peuples pour le suicide.
51	XI	(9)	Sur le plus ou moins de rigueur des peines corporelles chez différens peuples.
59	XII	(10)	De quelques peuples qui considèrent les coups comme des témoignages d'amour et d'amitié.
61	XIII	(11)	Considérations et détails sur la qualité évidemment mauvaise des alimens en Amérique.
63	XIV	(12)	Histoire succincte des opinions des peuples sauvages sur la nature de l'âme.
72	XV	(13)	Sur la ruse et la finesse de plusieurs peuples.
88			Sur les différens genres d'écriture (retouché à Lyon le 3 pluviôse an XII).
94	XVII	(15)	Histoire succincte des loix de la bienféance et la politesse parmi les peuples sauvages et à demi civilisés.
122	XVIII	(16)	Sur la chair de porc considérée comme aliment.
125	XIX	(17)	Sur la coutume de plusieurs peuples de dévorer la viande crue.
128	XX	(18)	Sur les idées des différens peuples par rapport à l'honneur et à la honte.
140	XXIV	(19)	Histoire succincte des opinions des peuples sauvages par rapport à la nature des animaux.
145	XXV	(20)	Sur la coutume qui existe chez quelques peuples de rendre la bouche difforme dans le dessein de l'embellir.
148	XXVI	(21)	Sur les mariages entre parens.
151	XXVII	(22)	Considérations sur l'influence des climats, et surtout de celui de la zone glaciale sur la santé de l'homme.
173	XII		Sur les causes du despotisme.
193	XXX	(26)	Sur l'état de nature.
201	XXXI	(27)	Idées des peuples sauvages touchant l'origine des hommes.

	207 I	(28)	Mémoires pour servir à l'histoire naturelle, morale et politique du genre humain. Sur les idées de différens peuples touchant l'importance de la virginité.
	217 II	(29)	Considérations sur la coutume de plusieurs peuples chez lesquels les hommes gardent le lit aux couches de leurs femmes; et sur les mutilations volontaires en usage chez plusieurs nations.
	224 XXII	(30)	Sur les nuits nuptiales chez différens peuples, avec quelques considérations sur les nuits et les années d'épreuve.
	236 XXXIII	(31)	Sur les mariages précoces chez différens peuples.
	238 XXXII	(i)	Sur les peines d'adultère chez différens peuples.
	245 XXXIII	(ii)	Sur l'usage des épiceries sous la zone torride.
	247 XXXIV	(iii)	Sur les causes de polygamie.
	255 XXXIV et dernier		Histoire succincte de la noblesse ou des distinctions héréditaires chez les divers peuples du monde.
	257		Idées des peuples sauvages sur la noblesse. [Reboul notes that he could not find the rest of this memoir.]

1.4 324 *Cours d'histoire naturelle de l'homme*, 2ᵉ race, 11ᵉ leçon (Asie Orientale).

342 *Cours d'histoire naturelle de l'homme*, 2ᵉ race, 12ᵉ leçon (Japon).

BIBLIOTHÈQUE DE LA FACULTÉ DE MÉDECINE DE PARIS

1.5 MS. *2197.13*
'Extrait d'un mémoire sur la force physique des sauvages de la Terre de Diemen, et de la Nouvelle-Hollande, et des inhabitants de Timor' by François Péron.

BIBLIOTHÈQUE DE L'INSTITUT DE FRANCE, PARIS

1.6 MS. *5651.3*
'Mémoire sur le Cap de Bonne-Espérance, présenté au gouvernement français, le 22 août 1801' by Marivault.
MS. *5651.7*
Péron's report to Comte Decaen on Port Jackson [a copy of the original in the Bibliothèque municipale de Caen, papiers Decaen, tome 92.]

BIBLIOTHÈQUE DU MUSÉUM D'HISTOIRE NATURELLE, PARIS

1.8 *MS. 1214.6*
'Rapport sur le voyage entrepris par les ordres du gouvernement, et sous la direction de l'Institut par le capitaine Baudin (3 nivôse an IX)' by the commission of the *Institut*.

1.9 *MSS. 1685–1689*
'Voyage de découvertes par le capitaine Baudin sur les corvettes le Géographe et le Naturaliste' par citoyen Riedlé, mort à Timor.

1.10 *MS. 2082*
Letters of Baudin to Jussieu and to Hamelin.

BIBLIOTHÈQUE NATIONALE, PARIS

1.11 *MS. 9439–9441*
Various documents pertaining to Baudin and the expedition to Australia, including a copy of his 'Journal de bord'.

1.12 *MS. 9373*
'Mémoire abrégé sur l'Inde en égard aux circonstances actuelles, présenté au directoire exécutif de la République française' by Lescallier.

1.13 *MS. 9407*. Papers on Bougainville.

Primary Published Sources

2.1 AUBRY publisher's catalogue for 26 messidor an IX, carries an announcement of Ravaut's *Correspondance littéraire et commerciale, ou annonces économiques des sciences, des arts, des lettres, du commerce et des découvertes utiles*, feuilleton périodique par une société de gens utiles.
[I have found no further trace of this periodical.]

2.2 BORY DE ST. VINCENT, Jean-Baptiste-Geneviève-Marcellin
Voyage dans les quatre principales îles des mers d'Afrique, Paris an XIII – 1804.

2.3 *Homo: essai zoologique sur le genre humain*, Paris 1827. (edited, with J.-J. Marcel and others).

2.4 *Histoire scientifique et militaire de l'expédition en Egypte*, Paris 1832.

2.5 BRITTON, Alexander, and BLADEN, F.M.
Historical Records of New South Wales, 7 volumes, Sydney 1893–1901.
[The appendix to volume 4 has translations of Baudin's letters to Governor King.]

2.6 BROSSES, Charles de
Histoire des navigations aux terres australes, Paris 1756.

2.7 CONDORCET, Marie-Jean-Antoine-Nicolas CARITAT, Marquis de
Réflexions sur l'esclavage des nègres, Neufchatel 1781.
[Published under the pseudonym Joachim SCHWARTZ.]

2.8 COURT DE GÉBELIN, Antoine
Le Monde Primitif analysé et comparé avec le Monde Moderne, 9 volumes, Paris 1773–1782.
[The spelling 'Gibelin' is also found.]

2.9 DEGÉRANDO, Joseph-Marie
Considérations sur les diverses méthodes à suivre dans l'observation des peuples sauvages, s.l.n.d.
[The title page of the 57-page book is headed: 'I: Société des Observateurs de l'Homme'. The date of publication can be inferred from the *imprimatur* at the end, which reads as follows: 'Extrait des procès-verbaux des séances de la Société des Observateurs de l'Homme. Sur la proposition d'un membre, la Société arrête que le Mémoire du citoyen DEGÉRANDO, intitulé: *Considérations sur les méthodes à suivre dans l'observation des Peuples Sauvages*, sera imprimé. Certifié conforme, à Paris, le 28 fructidor, an 8. *Signé*, L.-F. Jauffret, sécrétaire perpétuel de la Société.' The text appears to survive only in the Bibliothèque Nationale, Paris, but was reprinted with a brief anonymous comment, under the rubric: 'Documents anthropologiques: l'Ethnographie en 1800', in the *Revue d'Anthropologie*, IIᵉ série, tome VI, 1883, pp. 152–182.]

2.10 *Des signes et de l'art de penser considérés dans leurs rapports mutuels*, Paris an VIII.

2.11 *De la génération des connoissances humaines*, Berlin 1802.

2.12 *Histoire comparée des systèmes de philosophie relativement aux principes des connoissances humaines*, Paris 1804.

2.13 *Du perfectionnement moral, ou de l'éducation de soi-même*, Paris 1824.

2.14 *De l'éducation des sourds-muets de naissance*, Paris 1827.

2.15 *Des progrès de l'industrie, considérés dans leurs rapports avec la moralité de la classe ouvrière*, Paris 1841.

2.16 DÉMEUNIER, Jean-Nicolas
L'esprit des usages et des coutumes des différens peuples, ou observations tirées des voyageurs et des historiens, London and Paris, 1776.

2.17 JOMARD, E.-F. (ed.)
Description de l'Egypte, ou recueil des observations qui ont été faites en Egypte pendant l'expédition de l'armée française, 20 volumes, Paris 1809–1828.

2.18 LEMONTEY, Pierre-Edouard
Raison, folie, petit cours de morale mis à la portée des vieux enfans; suivi des Observateurs de la Femme, ed. III, Paris 1816. [The *Observateurs de la Femme* was published anonymously in 1803.]

MAGASIN ENCYCLOPÉDIQUE
A periodical publication edited by Millin, and a most useful place to see the ideas of the time in action:

2.19	an III	(1795)	tome I pp. 352–362	Questions d'économie politique par le citoyen Volney.
2.20	an IV	(1795)	tome IV p. 159	Review of MILLIN 2.41.
2.21	an VI	(1798)	tome II pp. 125–126	Letter on Degérando's memoir on signs.
2.22	an VII	(1798)	tome IV pp. 546 ff.	Report of the first meeting of the *Institut de Caire*.
2.23	an VII	(1799)	tome I pp. 115–116	Grégoire and the claim that negroes are not inferior to whites.
2.24			tome VI p. 187	The journey of Olivier to the Middle East.
2.25	an VIII	(1799)	tome V p. 458	On Jauffret, 'ami des enfans'.
2.26		(1800)	tome I pp. 408–410	Introduction of the *Société des Observateurs de l'Homme*.
2.27			p. 413	Baudin's expedition and astronomy.
2.28			tome III pp. 259–262	Baudin's farewell dinner.
2.29			pp. 531–532	First public meeting of the *Société des Observateurs de l'Homme*.
2.30			tome IV pp. 45–54	Note by Langlès on the commerce of Egypt.
2.31	an IX	(1801)	tome IV pp. 540–544	Report of a meeting of the *Société des Observateurs de l'Homme*.

2.32		tome V pp. 256–257	Degérando on 'le Sauvage d'Aveyron'.
2.33		pp. 265 ff.	Constitution of the Société des Observateurs de l'Homme.
2.34 an X	(1803) tome II	p. 537	Letter of Baudin to Jussieu.
2.35 an XI	(1803) tome IV	pp. 294 ff.	Review of MALLOUET 2.40 by Degérando.
2.36	(1808) tome IV	pp. 191 ff. 445 ff.	Review of PÉRON 2.43 by G.-J. Oberlin.
2.37	(1810) tome I	pp. 404–418	Review of RAYMOND 2.45.
2.38	(1813) tome I	pp. 338 ff.	Note on the Société africaine with the claim that negroes and whites differ only in colour.

2.39 MAINE DE BIRAN, Pierre-François Gonthier
Oeuvres, publiées par P. Tisserand, tome VI Paris 1930.
[p. 141: a letter including a description of Degérando.]
[see F. C. T. MOORE 3.17.]

2.40 MALLOUET, V.-P.
Collection de Mémoires et Correspondances officielles sur l'Administration des Colonies, et notamment sur la Guyanne françoise et hollandoise, Paris an X.

2.41 MILLIN, Aubin-Louis
Des variétés de l'espèce humaine, indiquées dans les poëmes d'Homère, Paris 1795.

2.42 PÉRON, François
Observations sur l'anthropologie etc., Paris, Imprimerie de la Stoupe, an VIII.
[This work is now lost.]

2.43 PÉRON, François and FREYCINET, Louis
Voyage de découvertes aux terres australes etc.,
vol. I (Péron), Paris 1807
vol. II (Péron, then Freycinet), Paris 1816
vol. III (Péron), Paris 1815
Atlas (Freycinet), Paris 1812.

2.44 PINKERTON, John
A general Collection of the best and most interesting Voyages and Travels in all Parts of the World, London 1814.

2.45 RAYMOND, G.-M.
Métaphysique des études, ou recherches sur l'état actuel des méthodes dans l'étude des lettres et des sciences, Paris an XII – 1804.

2.46 RAYNAL, Guillaume-Thomas-François
Histoire philosophique et politique des établissements et du commerce des Européens dans les deux Indes, Paris 1770.

2.47 REBOUL, Robert-Marie
Correspondance inédite de L.-F. Jauffret, Draguignan 1874.
[A limited edition of 100 copies.]

2.48 RÉMUSAT, Charles-François-Marie de
Politique libérale, ou fragments pour servir à la défense de la Révolution française, Paris 1860.

2.49 RICHARDSON, John
A Dissertation on the Languages, Literature and Manners of Eastern Nations, (ed. III), Oxford 1778.
[Chapter on women, pp. 330 ff.]

2.50 ROUSSEAU, Jean-Jacques
Emile, ou de l'Education, Amsterdam 1762.

2.51 SECONDAT, Charles-Louis de, baron de la Brède et de MONTESQUIEU
L'esprit des loix, 1748.

2.52 SMITH, Adam
An Enquiry into the Nature and Causes of the Wealth of Nations, Dublin 1776.
[French translations:
BLAVET, J.-L., London 1788 – Paris an IX
GARNIER, G., Paris an X – 1802.]

2.53 WAITZ, Theodor
Introduction to Anthropology, edited with additional notes of the author by J. F. Collingwood, London 1863.

2.54 WEBB, Beatrice
My apprenticeship, London 1926.

2.55 WHITE, John
Voyage to New South Wales, Botany Bay and Port Jackson, 1787-1789, translated with notes by Charles Pougens, Paris an III – 1795.

Secondary Sources

3.1 BARNWELL, P. J. and TOUSSAINT, A.
A short history of Mauritius, London 1949.

3.2 BOUTEILLER, M.
'La Société des Observateurs de l'Homme, ancêtre de la Société d'Anthropologie de Paris', in *Bulletins et Mémoires de la Société d'Anthropologie de Paris*, tome VIIe, X^e série, 1956, pp. 448-465.

3.3 BOUVIER, René and MAYNIAL, Edouard
Une aventure dans les mers australes: l'expédition du commandant Baudin (1800-1803), Paris 1947.

3.4 COOPER, H. M.
French exploration in South Australia, with especial reference to Encounter Bay, Kangaroo Island, The Two Gulfs and Murat Bay, 1802-1803, Adelaide 1952.
[Privately published in typescript edition of 200 copies.]

3.5 DUNMORE, John
French Explorers in the Pacific.
I. The Eighteenth Century, Oxford 1965.

3.6 DUPONCHEL, A.
Nouvelle Bibliothèque des voyages anciens et modernes, Paris s.d, [1841].
[Vol. VI, pp. 167-219, is an account of Baudin's voyage.]

3.7 FRAZER, Sir James George
Questions on the customs, beliefs and languages of Savages.
Cambridge 1907.

3.8 GIRARD, Maurice
François Péron, voyageur aux terres australes, Paris 1857.

3.9 GRILLE, F.
Louis de Freycinet: sa vie de savant et de marin, Paris 1853.

3.10 HANOTAUX, Gabriel and MARTINEAU, Alfred (ed.)
Histoire des colonies françaises et de l'expansion de la France dans le monde, vol. VI, Paris 1933.

3.11 HERVÉ, Georges
'Le premier programme d'anthropologie' in *Bulletins et Mémoires de la Société d'Anthropologie de Paris*, tome X, V^e série, 1909, pp. 473-487.

3.12 'Les premiers cours d'Anthropologie' in
Revue Anthropologique, 1914, pp. 255-276.

3.13 HODGEN, Margaret Trabue
Early Anthropology in the sixteenth and seventeenth centuries, Philadelphia 1964.

3.14 JOSÉ, Arthur W. and others
'Nicolas Baudin' in *Royal Australian Historical Journal and Proceedings*, vol. XX, 1934, part vi, pp. 337-396.

3.15 JULIEN, Ch.-André
La Politique Coloniale de la France sous la Révolution, le 1er Empire, et la Restauration, s.l.n.d. [typescript].

3.16 MAHAN, A. T.
The Influence of Sea-Power upon the French Revolution and Empire, 1793–1812, London 1892.

3.17 MOORE, F. C. T.
'Maine de Biran and Pestalozzi: some unpublished letters' in *Revue Internationale de Philosophie*, no. 75, 1966, pp. 27–52.

3.18 MURDOCK, George P. and others
Outline of Cultural Materials, ed. III, New Haven 1950.

3.19 PENNIMAN, T. K.
A hundred years of anthropology, ed. III, London 1965.

3.20 RADCLIFFE-BROWN, A. R.
Method in Anthropology, Chicago 1958.

3.21 REBOUL, Robert-Marie
L.-F. Jauffret, sa vie et ses oeuvres,
Paris/Marseille/Aix, 1869.

3.22 ROYAL ANTHROPOLOGICAL INSTITUTE
Notes and Queries on Anthropology, ed. VI, London 1951.

3.23 SEN, S. P.
The French in India, Calcutta 1958.

3.24 TRIEBEL, L. A.
'Péron in Tasmania' in *Papers and Proceedings of the Royal Society of Tasmania*, 1947, pp. 63–68.

INDEX

Index

The index is divided into two parts—of persons and of matters. Page numbers in heavy type mark references as especially important, giving, for example, bibliographic or biographic information. Names in heavy type appear as authors in the second and third sections of the bibliography.

I: PERSONS

A-Sam, 18, 28

Baudin, *Charles*, 40, 41
Baudin, *Nicolas-Thomas*, 5–43 *passim*, **8 ff.**, **27 ff.**, **34 ff.**, 56, 57, 60, 107, 110, 112, 115
Bernier, *Pierre-François*, 25, 33, 41
Bissy, 24, 25
Bligh, *Lieutenant William*, 33
Bonaparte, Napoleon, 9, 10, 23, 42, 44, 47, 48, 55
Bory de St. Vincent, *Jean-Baptiste-Geneviève-Marcellin*, 28, 56
Bouchaud, 46
Bougainville, *Louis-Antoine de*, 10, 13, 23, 24, 46, 65 n.
Buache, *Jean-Nicolas*, 22

Camus, 10
Chevalier, *Michel*, 51
Condillac, *Etienne Bonnot, abbé de*, 20
Cook, *James*, 46, 65 n., 95
Court de Gébelin, *Antoine*, 7

Cuvier, *Georges-Léopold-Chrétien-Frédéric-Dagebert*, 10, 17, **19**, 20, 21, 54, 57

Darquier, 23
Daubenton, *Louis-Jean-Marie*, 44
Decaen, *Charles-Matthieu-Isidore, comte*, **42**, 44, 109
Degérando, *Joseph-Marie*, ix, x, xi, **2 ff.**, 6, 8, 15, 17, 18, **19 f.**, 20, 30, 44, 45, 50, 52, 53, 54, 55, 57 f., 111, 112, 113
Demaimieux, 24
Démeunier, *Jean-Nicolas*, 7
Destutt de Tracy, *Antoine-Louis-Claude*, 47
Dolomieu, *Déodat-Guy-Silvain-Tancrède Gratet de*, 24
Durkheim, *Emile*, 1
Duteil, 10

Fleurieu, 9, 10, 22
Flinders, *Matthew*, 37

Forfait, 21, 22, 43
Fourcroy, *Antoine-François, comte de*, 23, 24
Frazer, *Sir James George*, 1, 5 n.
Freycinet, *Louis*, 40, 56

Garat, *Dominique-Joseph*, 20

Hallé, *Jean-Noël*, 19, 23, 24
Haller, 17
Hamelin, *Emanuel*, 22, 25, 34, 37, 40, 110

Jauffret, *Louis-François*, **7,** 8, **16,** 19, 21, 24, 44, **45, 46, 47,** 48, 50, 54, 107, 112, 114, 116
Jussieu, *Antoine-L. de*, 9, 10, 17, 19, 23, 25, 27, 34, 38, 40, 110, 113

Kéraudry, 21
King, *Governor Philip Gidley*, 37, 39

Lacépède, *Bernard-Germain-Etienne Delaville, comte de*, 9, 10, 19, 21, **44,** 45
Lamarck, *Jean-Baptiste-Pierre-Antoine de Monnet, Chevalier de*, 19
Langlès, 10, 112
La Pérouse, *Jean-François de Galaup, comte de*, 22
Laplace, *Pierre-Simon, marquis de*, 10
Leblond, 24
Legout, 46
Lelièvre, 10
Lemontey, *Pierre-Edouard*, 7, 49

Lescallier, **13,** 110
Leschenault de la Tour, 41
Levaillant, *François*, 19, 23, 60
Le Villain, *Stanislaus*, 33
Lharidon, 25, 26
Locke, *John*, 20

Magallon, *General*, 26 f.
Maine de Biran, *Pierre-François Gonthier*, **54 f.,** 57, 116
Malinowski, *Bronislaw*, 1
Mallouet, *V.-P.*, 50, 113
Marivault, **14,** 109
Maugé, *René*, 22, 23, 25, 34, 36
Meifredy, *fils de Louis*, 23
Michaux, *André*, 22, 28
Milbert, *J.-G.*, 25
Millin, *Aubin-Louis*, 17, 19, 24
Murdock, *George P.*, 5 n.

Nelson, *David*, 33

Olivier, 12, 112

Patrin, *Eugène-Louis-Melchior*, 17, 18, 23
Péron, *François*, **20 f.,** 25 f., **29 ff., 34,** 36, **38,** 42 ff., 46, 47, 49, 50, 56, 57, 109, 113, 115, 116
Pestalozzi, *Heinrich*, 54, 116
Pfeffel, 46
Pinel, *Philippe*, 17, 23
Pinkerton, *John*, 7
Portalis, *Jean-Etienne-Marie*, 17, 23
Portalis, *jnr.*, 18
de Puche, 25, 30, 33

Raymond, G.-M., 54, 113
Rémusat, *Charles-François-Marie de*, 52
Richardson, *John*, 18
Riedlé, *Anselme*, 22, 23, 33, 34, 36, 110
Rousseau, *Jean-Jacques*, 15, 18, 54

Sautier, *Antoine*, 33
Sicard, *Roch-Ambroise Cucurron, abbé*, 17, 19, 46, 72

Smith, *Adam*, 14, 39, 49
Ste.-Beuve, *Charles-Augustin*, 57
St. Hilaire, *Geoffroy de*, 19
St.-Pierre, *Jacques-Bernadin-Henri de*, 21

Thouin, *André*, 23
Triebel, L. A., 34
Tylor, *Sir Edward B.*, 1

Webb, *Beatrice*, 51 f.
White, *John*, 15

II: MATTERS

Adultery, 90 f., 109
Animals, 35, 95, 108
Anthropology, 19, 21, 24, 33
    comparative, 5, **62 ff.**
    physical, 4, 19, 45
    social, 4, 7, 88–101, *passim*
Antilles
    see West Indies
Association of Ideas, 70, 72, **84**
Attention, 86
Australian expedition, x, 2, 7, 8, 9, 10, 15, 20, **25–41**, 110, 113, 115
Aveyron,
    'le sauvage d'Aveyron', 113

Bora ground, 29, 36

Cannibalism, 79
Cope of Good Hope, 8, 14, 109
Climate, 62, **78**

Clothes, 66, **79**
Colonies, x, 6, **13**, 39, 43, 44, 50, 57, 103, 115
Commerce, x, 5, 10, 11, **12 ff.**, 16, 23, 38, 39, 46, 57, **97**, 103, 112, 114
Crime, 94

Divorce, 90
Dreams, 79

Economics, 4, 10, **51 f.**, 95–98, 112, 114
Education, 54, **55 ff.**, 66, 91, 111, 114
    of deaf-mutes, 54, **72**, 111
    see Physical education
Egoism, 61
Egyptian expedition, 11, **12**, 110, 111
Espionage, **13 ff.**, **42 ff.**, 109, 110

Family, 4, **88**, 90, 91

Foresight, 86
Food, 21, **78**, 107, 108, 109
Friendship, 32, 98, 108

Gesture, 72, 108

History and anthropology, 1, 5, 46, 63
Hottentots, 14

Idéologie, 47
Ile de France
 see Mauritius
Illness, 80
Imagination, **85 f.**
Imbecility, 80
India, 13, 114, 116
Industry, 95 f.
Insanity, 80
Institut de Caire, **11**, 19, 112
Institut de France, 9, 10, **11**, 13, 15, 18, 19, 22, 24, 57, 107, 110

Kinship, 4, **89**

Language, x, **2 f.**, 63, 64, **67, 68 ff.**, **70 ff.**
Legend, 5, 100
Longevity, 81
Love, 89 f., 108

Magasin Encyclopédique, 15 f., 17, 20, 23, 50, 58, 112
Malays, 31 f.
Marriage, **90 f.**, 108, 109
Mauritius, 25, **26–29**, 37, 39, 41, 42, 49, 114
Memory, 86
Menstrual Periods, 90

Modesty, 89
Muséum d'Histoire Naturelle, 9, 10, 110

Needs, 79, 84
New Guinea, 29, 39, 41
Numbers, 76

Participation in native societies, x, 2, 63 f., 70
Perth, 29
Physical education, 80 f.
Physical strength, 38, **78**, 109
Political systems, **91 f.**, 94, 108
Port Jackson
 see Sydney
Property, 32, 94
Pyramids, 63

Reflection, 86
Religion, 4, **84 f.**, 98, **99 f.**, 108

Sensations, 4, 82
'Sickness of a time', **51 ff.**, 54, 56
Slavery, 6, **26 f.**, **49 f.**, 56, 111
Sleep, 78 f.
Social phenomena as having meaning, 3, **62**, 69, 77, 100
Société africaine, 113
Société de l'Afrique intérieure, **22 ff.**
Société pour l'amélioration de l'éducation élémentaire, 53
Société des amis des noirs, 6
Société d'encouragement pour l'industrie nationale, 53

Société des Observateurs de l'Homme, 2, 7, 8, **17,** 18, 19, 20, 22, 24, 44, 45, 47, 48, 49, 50, 112, 113
State of Nature, 6, 88, 108, 113
Suicide, 108
Sydney, **37,** 38, 39, 109

Tasmania, **28 f.,** 38, 39, 109, 116
Tenerife, 8, 25
Theft, 32, 67
Timor, 29, **30 ff.,** 38, 41, 109
Traditions, 69, 108
Trinidad, 8

'Useful knowledge', **52 ff.,** 110

Van Diemen's Land
see Tasmania

War, **92 ff.**
West Indies, 8
Women, 18, **89,** 114
Writing, 76 f., 107, 108